COPYRIGHT

C000107987

Table of Contents

Table of Contents

In questions 'Odd One Out' , you could follow the **<u>common rule</u>** between the shapes, and then, you can figure out the odd shape. This will be the shape the does not adhere to the rules

 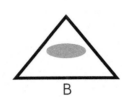 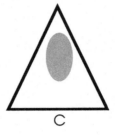 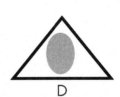

A	B	C	D

Common rule: *size of the triangle*

In the given example above, the common rule between all four shapes is the size of the triangle. So option C would be the odd one out, as it's shape does not adhere with the rule.

As you can observe, the eclipse is placed as a distractor and does not form part of the common rule. You must ignore any distractor properties.

Tip for Odd One Out questions: Concentrate on finding the **COMMON RULE**

 ## Approach

1

Have a full look at your options, think about what the common rules could possibly be. In an easy problem, you might be able to identify it immediately.

if the answer isn't as easy to find as the example given above, draw back to your list of common rules.

2 Remember the mnemonic ***Never Sneak Snack To A Crowded Picnic!*** *and try to find a common rule by using one of these properties.*

Never Sneak Snack To A Crowded Picnic!

| Number | Size | Shape | Total | Angle | Colour | Pattern |

Let us use the TOTAL property and see if we could identify a common rule in this example:

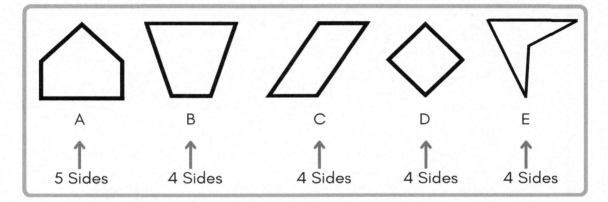

A	B	C	D	E
↑ 5 Sides	↑ 4 Sides	↑ 4 Sides	↑ 4 Sides	↑ 4 Sides

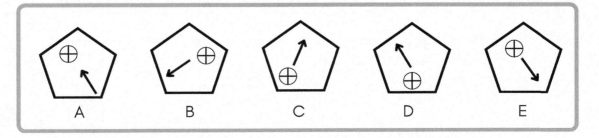

The common rule in the given example is that all the shapes have 4 sides in total. Option A doesn't fit the common rule so it must be the odd one out!

3 Sometimes all of the choices will appear very similar to each other. So looking for appearance rule like we did on the previous example is likely not going to be of help.

A   B   C   D   E

When the appearance is almost similar, always look for the extra rule: the Position Rule.

 To remember features relating to the **POSITION OF ELEMENTS** use the mnemonic '**M.O.P.S.**'

Movement **O**rientation, **P**lacement, **S**ymmetry

 Top Tip: When there's an arrow in the question, it's most likely going to be position question.

Let's look at the way the arrow is pointing.

A   B   C   D   E

The common rule in this example is that the arrow is pointing away from the circle, but Option A does not follow that rule!

(4) If you have tried all the previous steps, and you've still haven't figured its rule, now you should look for a **RULE SYSTEM**. This is a rule where two or more rules are used to create a common rule.

In the given example, the relevant features are **colour** and number.

If the shape inside is **grey stripes**, there are two small shapes at the top, but if the inner shape is **black stripes**, there are three!

That is the 4 step process that'll guide you to solve every questions in the Odd One Out!

 # Example Question

A   B   C   D   E

1 Let's begin by looking for **APPEARANCE-BASED** attributes.

Each image is composed of **one white arrowhead, one large white square** (with either round or pointy corners) and **one smaller grey or black shape.**

2 Now, let us think about the **POSITION-BASED** attributes!

In every image, the arrow always points to the **top-left corner** of the box.

3 Examine if all the images **share** these position and appearance attributes.

 The **colour** of the small shape (grey or black) does not follow any pattern. This means it is designed to confuse you, we call it **red herring.**

In all of the images, the arrow pointing towards the top left corner, has a curved edge. However, in B, the arrow only has straiht edges.

B is the odd one out!

4

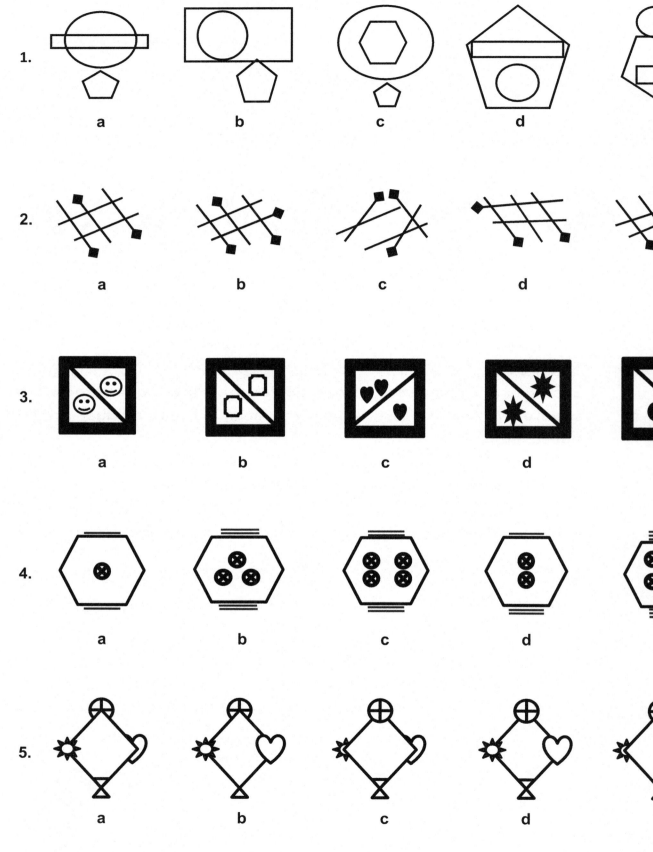

1.

    a   b   c   d   e

2.

    a   b   c   d   e

3.

    a   b   c   d   e

4.

    a   b   c   d   e

5.

    a   b   c   d   e

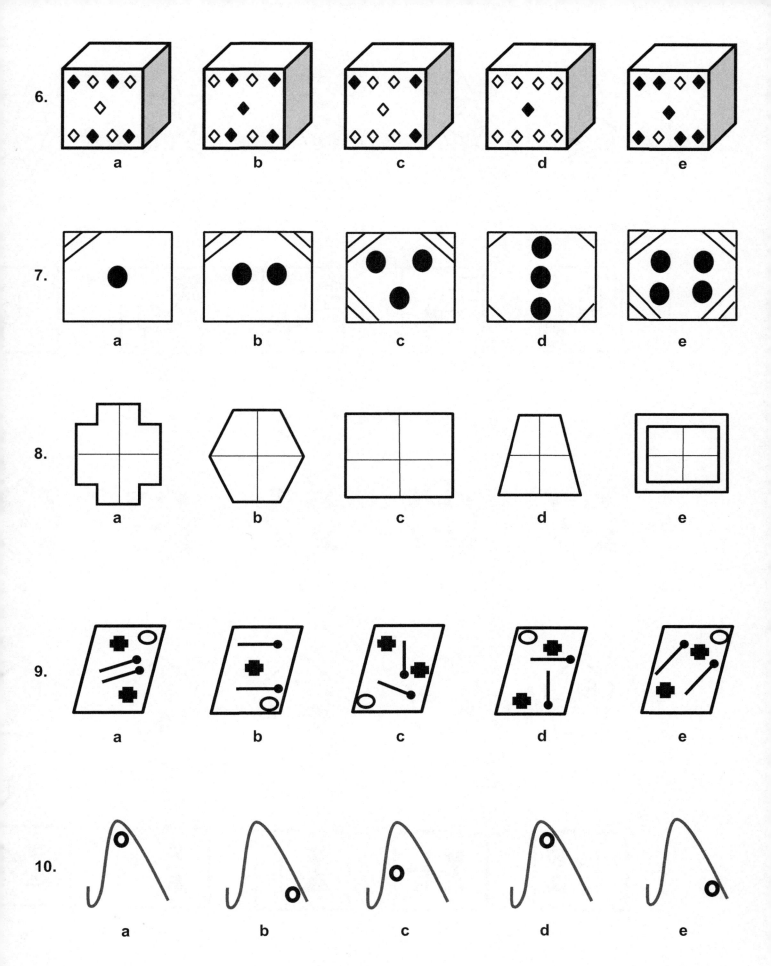

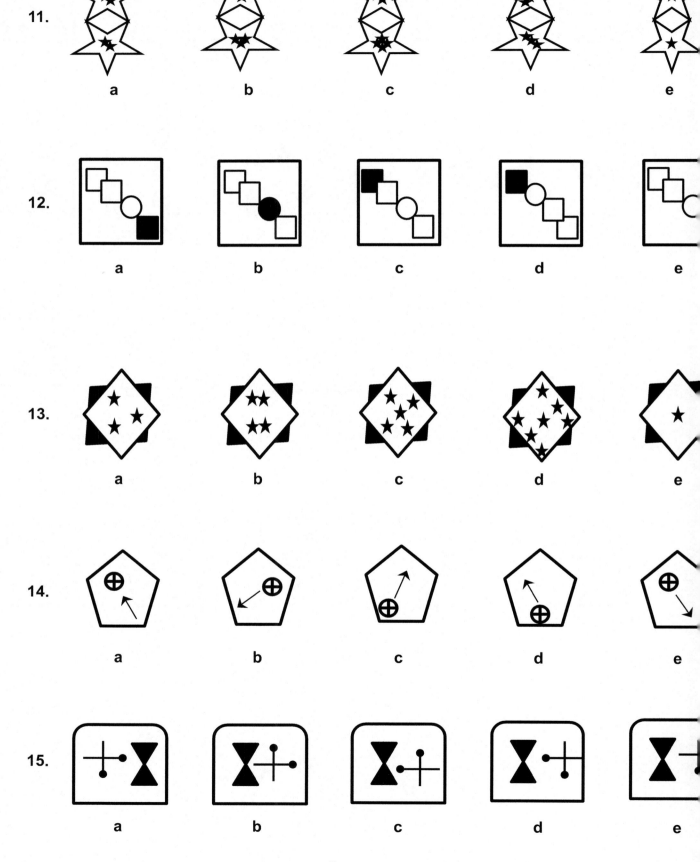

11.   a   b   c   d   e

12.   a   b   c   d   e

13.   a   b   c   d   e

14.   a   b   c   d   e

15.   a   b   c   d   e

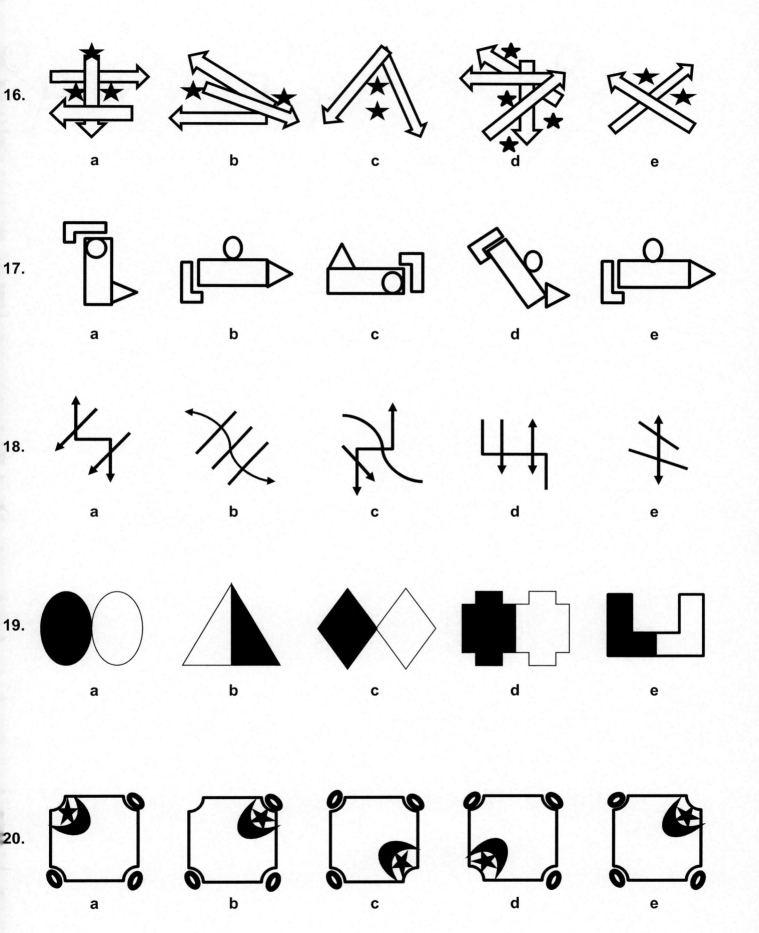

16. a   b   c   d   e

17. a   b   c   d   e

18. a   b   c   d   e

19. a   b   c   d   e

20. a   b   c   d   e

8

21.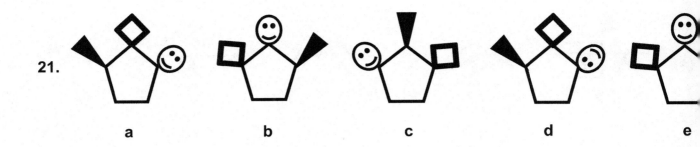

a   b   c   d   e

NVR TYPE 2: SIMILARITIES

In questions of similarities , you have to identify the common features among the **special group** of images or shapes. These common features will become the **common rule** in order to join this special group.

You are then given a new set of test shapes of which you must identify the one that can join the special group.

Example: Which among these test shape on the right belong to the special group on the left?

The Special Group

Test Shape A   **Test Shape B**   **Test Shape C**

Common rules:
1. Black Triangle
2. Arrow pointing to the triangle.

So to join the group, you should *follow* these two rules.

Choose one test shape from the choices above that can join the special group of shapes on the left.

(1) Remember the mnemonic **'Never Sneak Snack To A Crowded Picnic!'**

Number **Size** **Shape** **Total** **Angle** **Colour** **Pattern**

Rule 1 *Colour / Shape:* The Black Triangle has to be present in the shape.

Rule 2 *Position:* The Arrow must be present and should be pointing to the black triangle.

2

Using the isolate and eliminate technique, check each rule and narrow down your options.

Rule 1: You can eliminate Test Shape C because the colour of its triangle is white instead of black.
Rule 2: You can eliminate Test Shape A because its arrow is pointing away from the traingle.

This leaves you with the answer Test Shape B.

 Remember: If it looks like there could be more than one answer, there's a possibility that you have **missed** one of the shared attributes! Keep looking until you identify **all** the attributes that connect the pair.

Look out! Some attributes might be associated to each other by a **rule.** In this example, there must be the **same number** of small circles as there are sides.

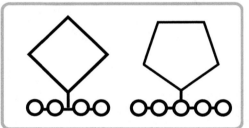

Example Question

If a common rule does not stand out to you immediately, break the shapes down into smaller pieces.

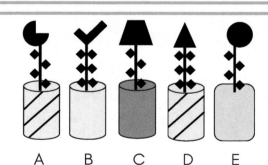

A   B   C   D   E

 First, look at the base. Perhaps there's a rule there?

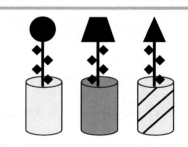 The options all have a cylindrical base, so that eliminates E!

11

Then look at the shapes on the stem: all of them have 4 diamonds attached to it.

That eliminates options B and D!

Now, all that's left are options A and C which seem to follow all the rules. This indicates that there's likely a **rule system** in place too.

Next, look at the top shape: Is there a rule between the circle, trapezium, and triangle?

It may seem like they have nothing in common at first. But, remember the mnemonic **"Never Sneak Snacks To A Crowded Picnic"**

When we try each of these properties on the top shape, we find they all have a vertical line of symmetry.

That eliminates option A which leaves us with the answer C!

C

NVR: Similarities

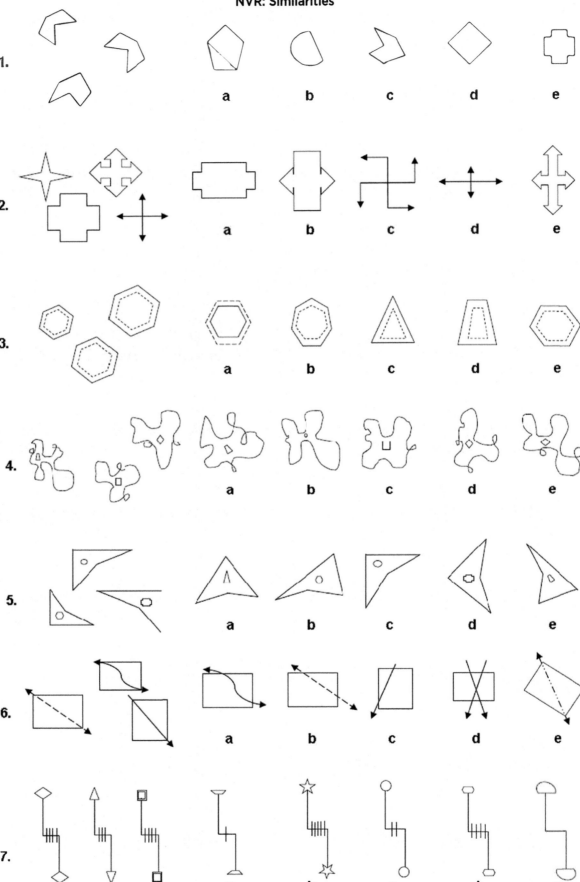

1. 　　　　　　　a　　b　　c　　d　　e

2. 　　　　　　　a　　b　　c　　d　　e

3. 　　　　　　　a　　b　　c　　d　　e

4. 　　　　　　　a　　b　　c　　d　　e

5. 　　　　　　　a　　b　　c　　d　　e

6. 　　　　　　　a　　b　　c　　d　　e

7. 　　　　　　　a　　b　　c　　d　　e

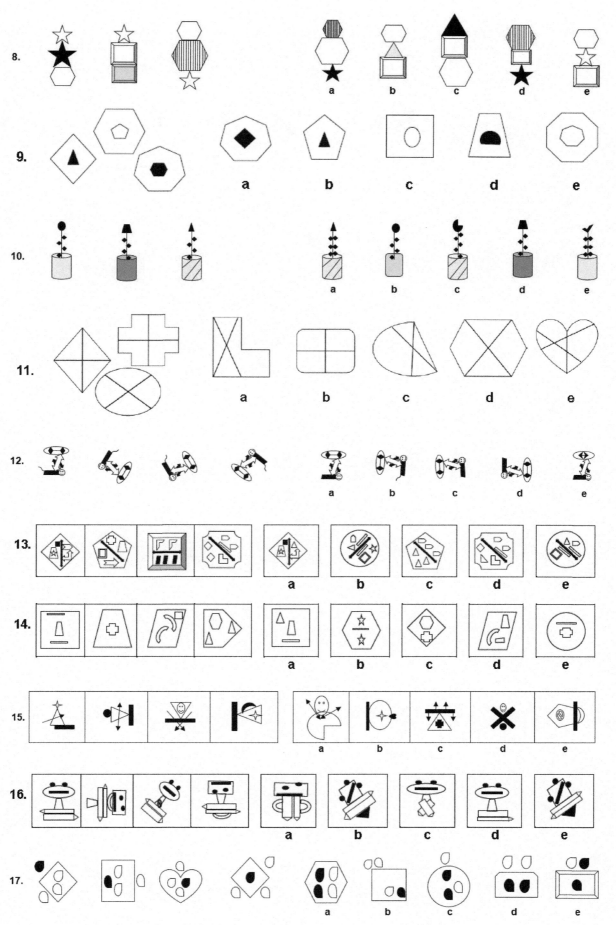

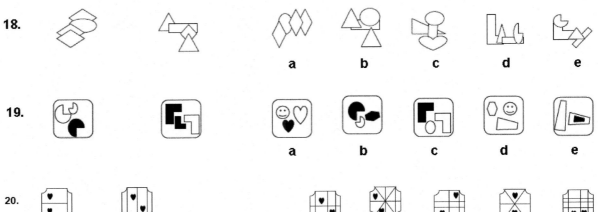

18.

19.

20.

NVR TYPE 3: REFLECTIONS

Reflection NVR can be its own type of question, or can come as one of the NVR properties (S– Symmetry). Here are some things to watch out for when solving reflection questions:

- The reflected shape must be the same size as the original shape.
- The reflection could be across a horizontal or vertical line, choose the relevant option.
- The shading does not change for horizontal and vertical stripes.
- All other shapes will be flipped over.

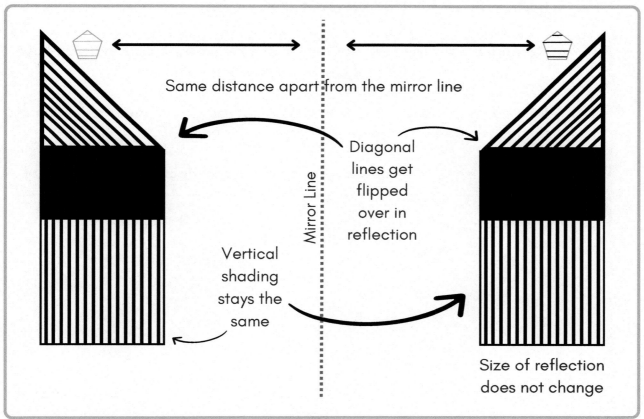

Reflection across a diagonal:

In this example, the object is rotated by 90°

(i.e. a quarter turn)

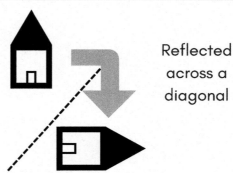

Reflected across a diagonal

1 Analyze the main shape you have. Identify all the **elements** that make up the shape. Consider: **colour, number, pattern** and **angles.**

2 **Rule out** any given answer choices that are **obviously incorrect.**

Are they **missing** any of the elements you identified?

3 Imagine a mirror **below, to the side,** or **an angle positioned next to** the main image or shape. What you would see in the mirror is how the main image or shape should look if it was reflected across a positioned at **horizontal, vertical, or diagonal line.**

4 **Compare** the answer option left to the reflected shape that you have imagined. Check if **all** of the elements have been reflected.

Rule out any answer options that does not show the correct reflection of the main image or shape.

You must be left with **one** answer option that **reflects the main shape!**

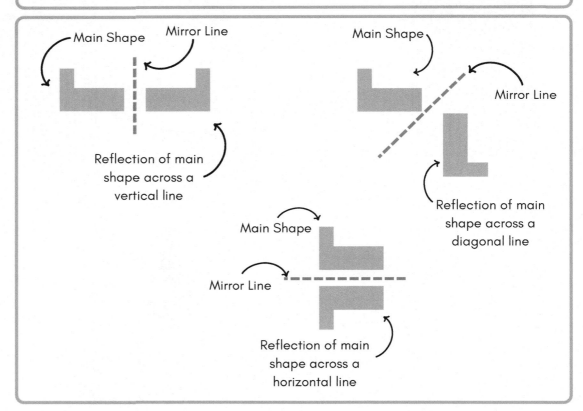

Example Question

Which of the following options below is a reflection of the main shape?

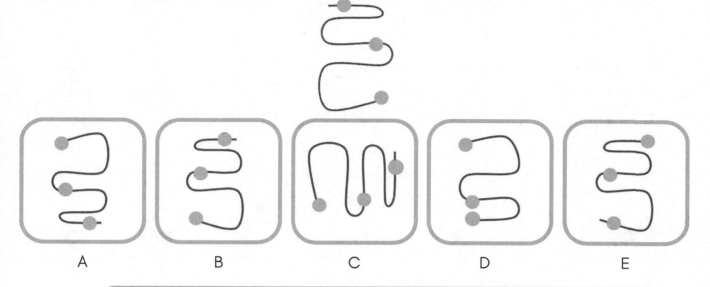

A   B   C   D   E

1 Look at the main shape...
- The main shape is made up of a line that has four bends and 3 small orange circles.

2 Are any of the options obviously incorrect?
- Option D is the **wrong shape.** The line only has three bends, compared to the main shape which has four bends.
- Option C is obviously a **rotation** of the main shape!

3 Take a look at the remaining options...
- Option A might seem like it could be a reflection of the main shape across a horizontal line, but it actually a **180° rotation** of the main shape.
- Options B and E are what's left.
- Can you see any difference between the two choices?
- The small circles are **placed differently!**
- We can then rule out Option E – which is a **red herring**! The circles are **positioned wrong.**

4 Answer:
- The correct answer is Option B!
- It is the **only** option that shows a **reflection** of the main shape – the shape is reflected across a vertical line.

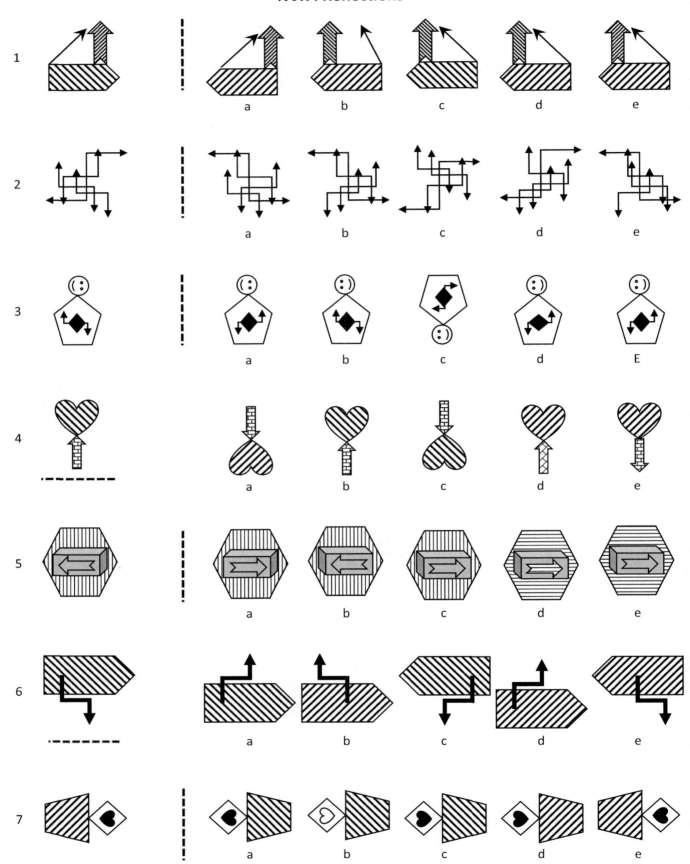

1

    a   b   c   d   e

2

    a   b   c   d   e

3

    a   b   c   d   E

4

    a   b   c   d   e

5

    a   b   c   d   e

6

    a   b   c   d   e

7

    a   b   c   d   e

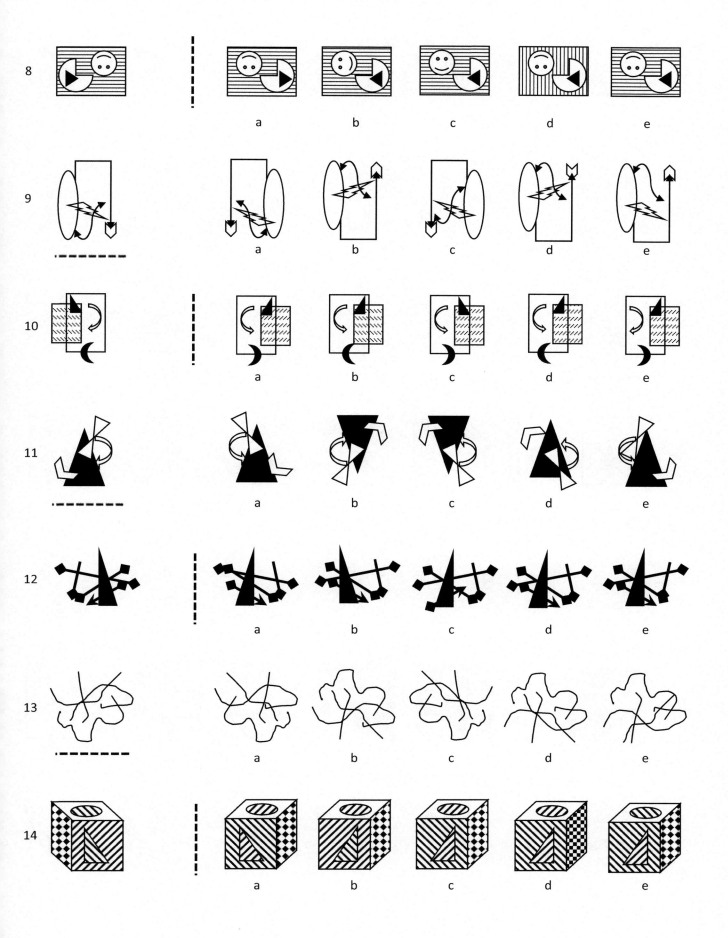

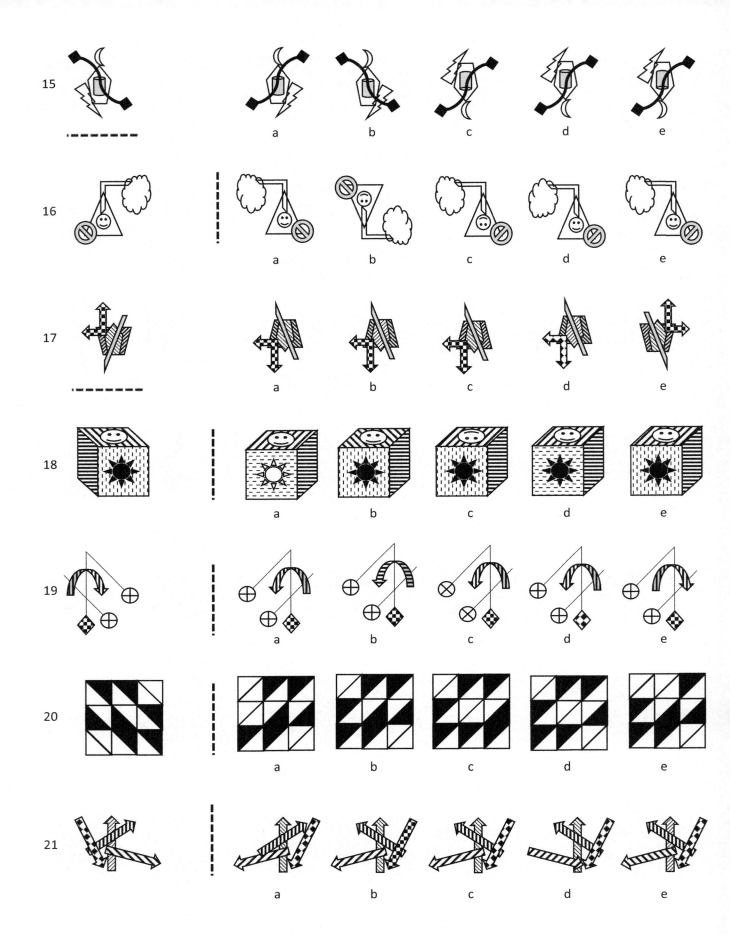

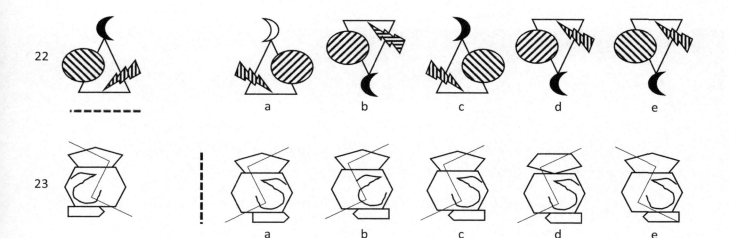

22

23

Rotation NVR can come as its own type of question, or appear as one of the NVR attributes (A - Angle of rotation) to consider in solving a question. In either case, you should note the following:

- The shape itself doesn't change in size nor do any features.
- Shape can be rotated clockwise or anti-clockwise.
- The shape can be turn by a quarter turn, half turn or three-quarters turn.

The best way to visualize the rotation is by the hands of the clock.

Currently, the hands of the clock is facing 3 o'clock, and is about to moved as shown in the arrow.

After a quarter turn clockwise was made, the clock hand faces o'clock.

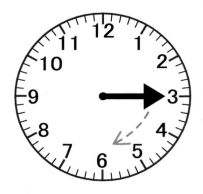

Also, don't forget that the shape itself does not change in terms of size and features. As you can see in the sample image below, the string is still tied to the right index finger.

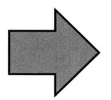

Rotated quarter turn clockwise

Hand is facing 10 o'clock

Hand is facing 2 o'clock

23

1 Look closely at the main shape provided. Identify all the **elements** that make up the shape, consider **colour, number, pattern** and **angles.**

2 **Rule out** any given answer choices that are **obviously incorrect.**
- Are they **missing** any of the elements you identified?
- Have the elements of the shape provided been **rotated by different amounts?**

3 Imagine what would the main image look like when it's **rotated.**

What would it look like when you turn the point around?

4 Compare the remaining options to the **rotated shape** you have imagined. Check if **all** of the **elements** have been correctly rotated. If a shape is striped, have the stripes been rotated in the same manner as the outline of the shape?

Rule out any options that do not show the correct rotation of the main image or shape. You should be left with **one option** that is the correct answer with the **correct rotation of the main image or shape!**

Watch out for stripes! The rotation of the shape's outline must be the same with the stipes.

main shape

45°
clockwise

90°
clockwise

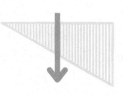
180°
clockwise

90°
clockwise

Which of the option is a rotation of the main shape?

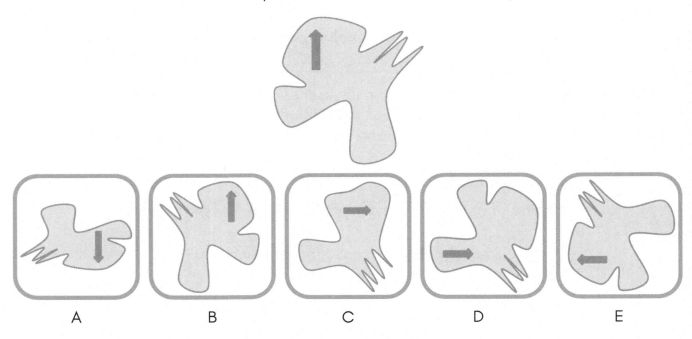

A   B   C   D   E

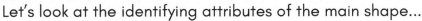

1 Let's look at the identifying attributes of the main shape...
- The main shape is an irregular grey shape composed of three large rounded extensions and three small triangular spikes.
- You can see an arrow in the largest rounded extension of the main shape.

2 Are any of the option obviously-incorrect?
- They grey outer shape in option A has the **wrong proportions** – it looks like a pressed version of the main shape.
- Option C is a **different shape** at all. It has four small triangular spikes instead if three and it is missing a rounded extension.
- Option B is more of a **reflection** of the main shape across a vertical line rather than a rotation.

3 Let's check the remaining options...
- Option D looks like it can be a 90° clockwise rotation of the main shape, but the placement of the arrow is **wrong,** it should be on the left of the spikes!

4 Answer:
- The correct answer is option **E,** it is the main shape in a **90° anticlockwise rotation.**

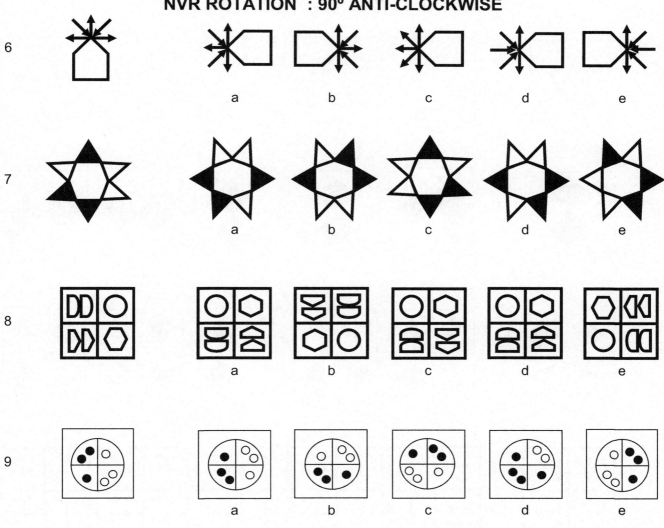

6

a   b   c   d   e

7

a   b   c   d   e

8

a   b   c   d   e

9

a   b   c   d   e

10

a   b   c   d   e

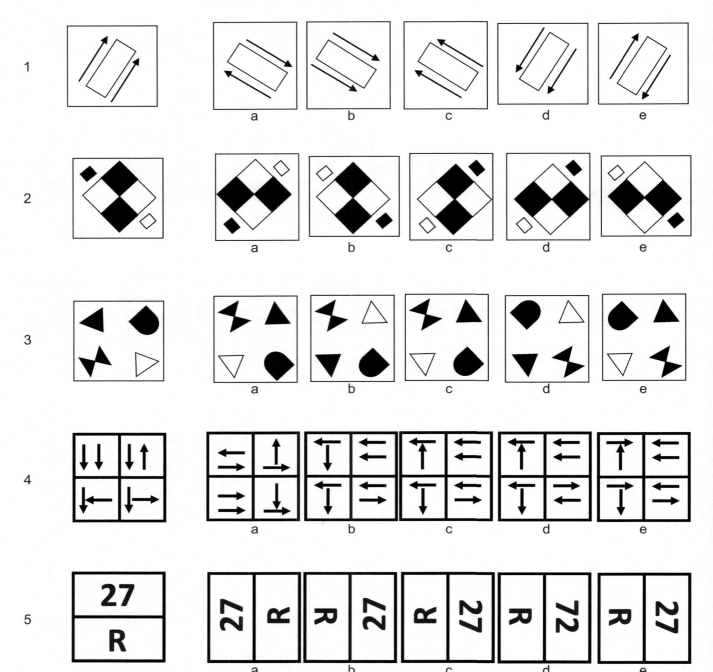

NVR TYPE 5: ANALOGY

In Analogy questions, you will be shown two pairs of images, one complete and one incomplete.

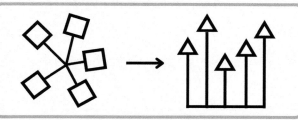 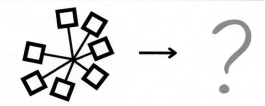

In each set of images, the first image is changed into the second image by following a **rule**. You should figure out the rule used and select the image which correctly completes the second set.

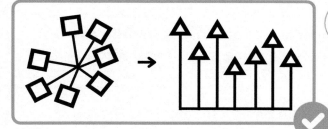

All the squares became triangles!

Approach

1   Identify several **attributes** in the images that could be used to **form a rule.**

In this example, **colour, shape** and **positions** seems like relevant features!

Use the mnemonic **Never Sneak Snack To A Crowded Picnic!** as your guide on important attributes to look for.

Never Sneak Snack To A Crowded Picnic!

Number | Size | Shape | Total | Angle | Colour | Pattern

Use the mnemonic **'M.O.P.S.'** to remember attributes relating to the **position of elements** - *M*ovement *O*rientation, *P*lacement, *S*ymmetry.

2 Come up with a set of **rules** that describe how the first image of each pair is **transformed** into the second image.

Shape:
- A three-layered shape turns into a column of three circles.

Colour & Position:
- The colour of the **outer layer** is the same as the **top circle.**
- The colour of the **middle layer** is the same as the **middle circle.**
- The colour of the **inner layer** is the same as the **inner circle.**

3 **Test out the rules** you came up with and try to finish the second pair of images using the options given.

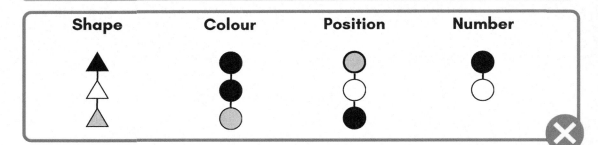

Shape | Colour | Position | Number

You must be left with **one option.**

If you are left with **none or more than one option**, try a different rule!

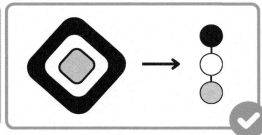

Which of the image below fits as a pair with the third image?

 →  :  → ?

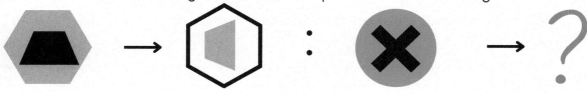

A   B   C   D   E

1 First, look for **attributes** that describe the transformation.

2 **Attributes** that might be relevant includes: **shape, orientation, size** and **position.**

Using these **attributes,** create **rules** about how the first image of each pair is **transformed** into the second image.

- **Size and Position:** The size and position of the shapes do not change.
- **Orientation:** Both shapes are rotated 90 degrees anti-clockwise
- **Shading:** The larger shape switches to a black outline, whereas the inner shape switches to the colour of the outer shape.

3 Use the isolate and eliminate technique and check each rule to narrow down your options.

 We can rule out...
- **A** because it has a hexagon rather than a circle.
- **B** because the larger shape is still coloured.
- **C** because the X hasn't changed colour.

E is a **red herring!** If we look closely, we can see that shading is the wrong way around. The X should be coloured.

A is the correct answer! It is the only option that can finish the second pair.

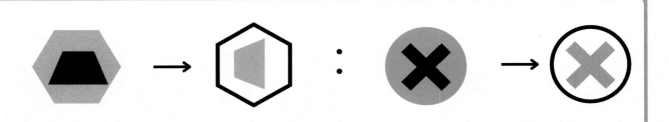

NVR – Analogy

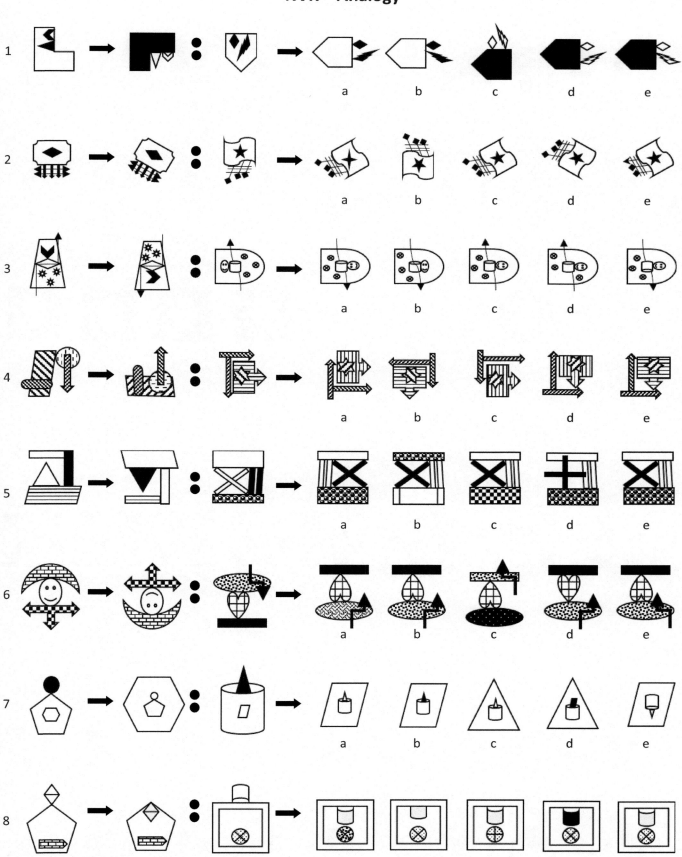

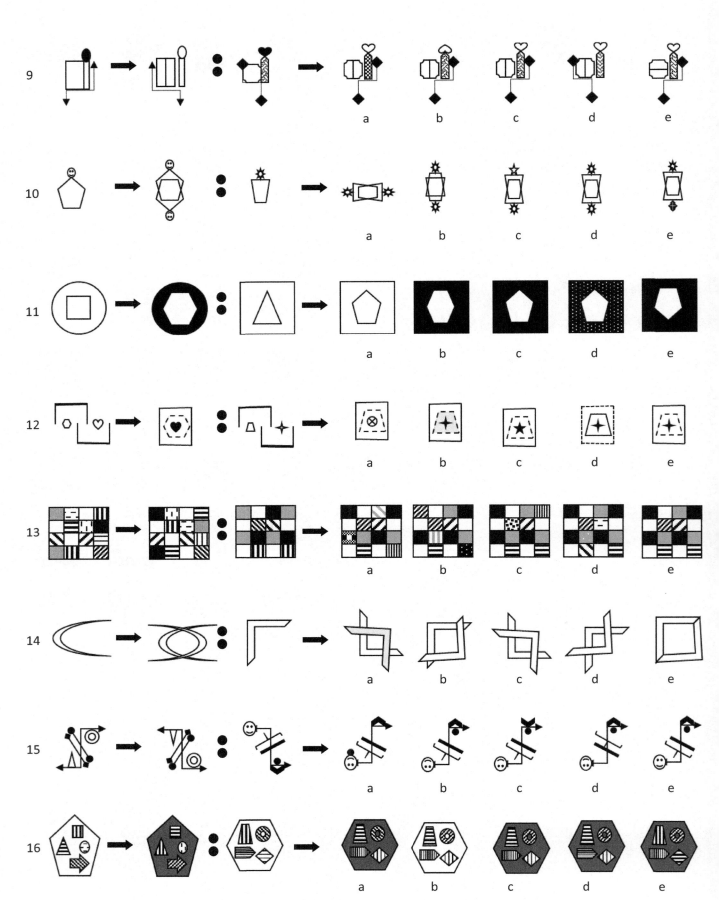

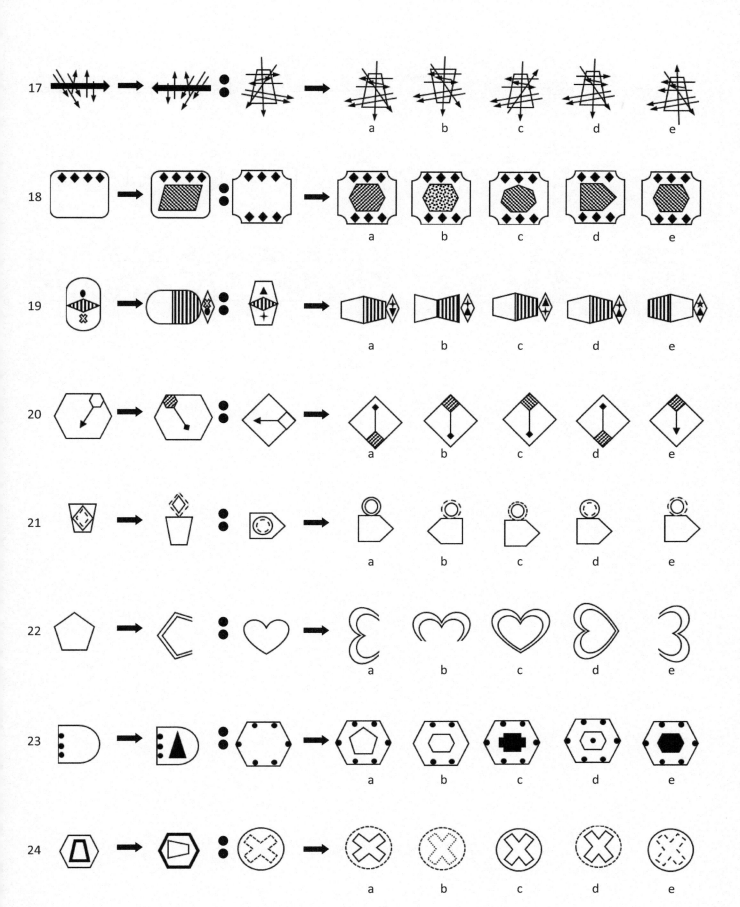

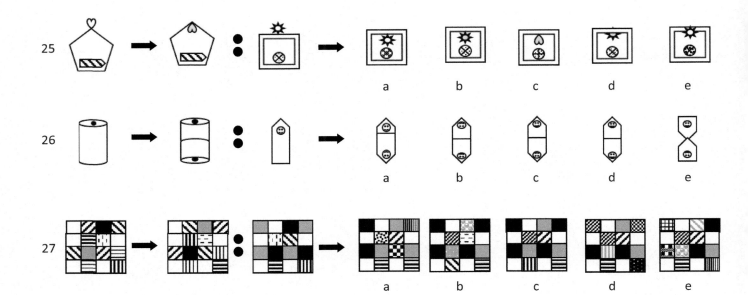

In **sequences** questions you will be given an incomplete sequence of image. You will have to choose your answer from the given options you complete the gap(s) in the sequence.

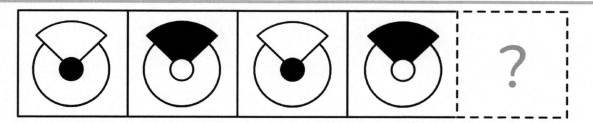

There will be rules that each shape follows when it changes from shape to shape.

These rules are likely to follow the appearance or properties rule we've discussed already.

Never Sneak Snacks To A Crowded Picnic!

Number	Size	Shape	Total	Angle	Colour	Pattern

M.O.P.S. - Movement Orientation, Placement, Symmetry

In the sequence of shapes, the following points are also very common:
1. **Movement of a shape**
2. **A Repeating Pattern**
3. **Adding or Taking away of a Shape**
4. **A combination of the above mentioned.**

Find the shape that completes the gap.

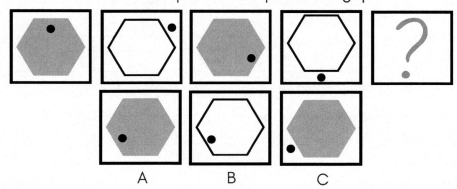

1 Always take it one rule at the time, and eliminate options that doesn't follow the rules.

 2 We find that every other shape the **shading pattern** changes. This means the gap will have a black shape, so that eliminates option B.

 3 The black dot is switching between going inside and going outside the shape, this means the black dot will be inside the shape, so this eliminates option C

We now know that the correct answer is option A, and we didn't have to find the last rule!

The third rule is that the black dot moves along the hexagon's sides! (Position)

🏆 Top Tips

 Focus on **one attribute at a time** and see how it changes between each step. If there is no obvious pattern, it could be a **red herring** (an attribute to distract you).

 Remember, **patterns** can reach different numbers of steps and may **reverse!**

 Once a **pattern** has started to repeat, there will likely be **identical attributes.** You can use this to quickly discover what any missing steps look like!

Which of the option will complete this sequence?

A   B   C   D   E

1 First, Identify the **attributes** that changes at each step. Use this to form a **pattern.**

2 **Rotation** - the total number of shapes is always three, but they rotate clockwise each step to form three different formations.

Pattern - the checkered patter rotates clockwise while the diagonal line pattern is always behind it (clockwise). It's also always the same three patterns.

Using these rules, try to eliminate some of the options given.

3 **Rotation** - since the 5th option in the series has the same formation as the 1st, we can assume that the rotation pattern is restarting on the 5th option. So the gap (in 4th place) will have a new formation. This eliminates option A, B and E.

Pattern - The patterns are always the same (Checkered, Horizontal line and diagonal line) throughout the sequence, this lets us eliminate option C, which does not have a horizontal lined pattern.

Option D is the correct answer! It is the only option that can complete the sequence without breaking any of the rules.

✓

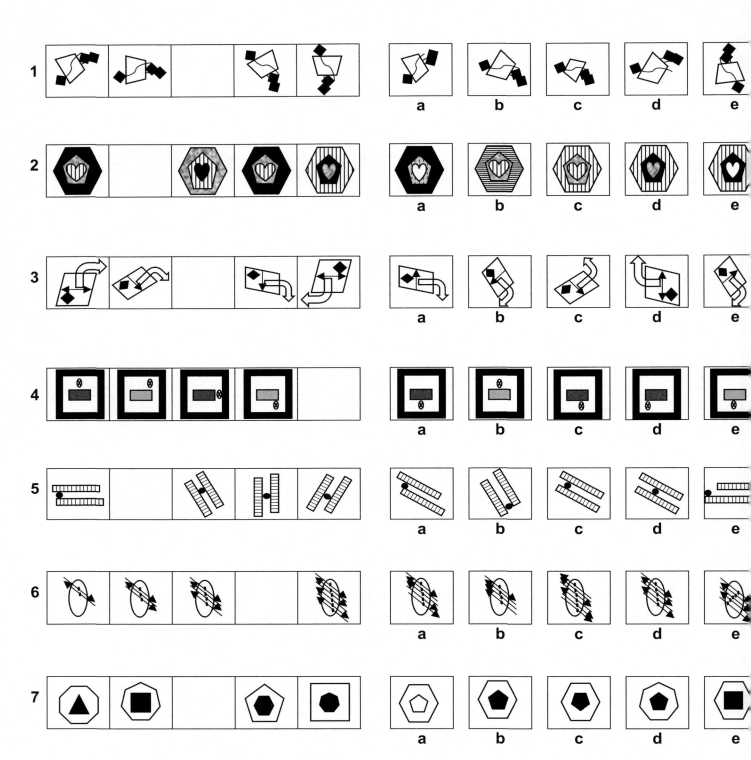

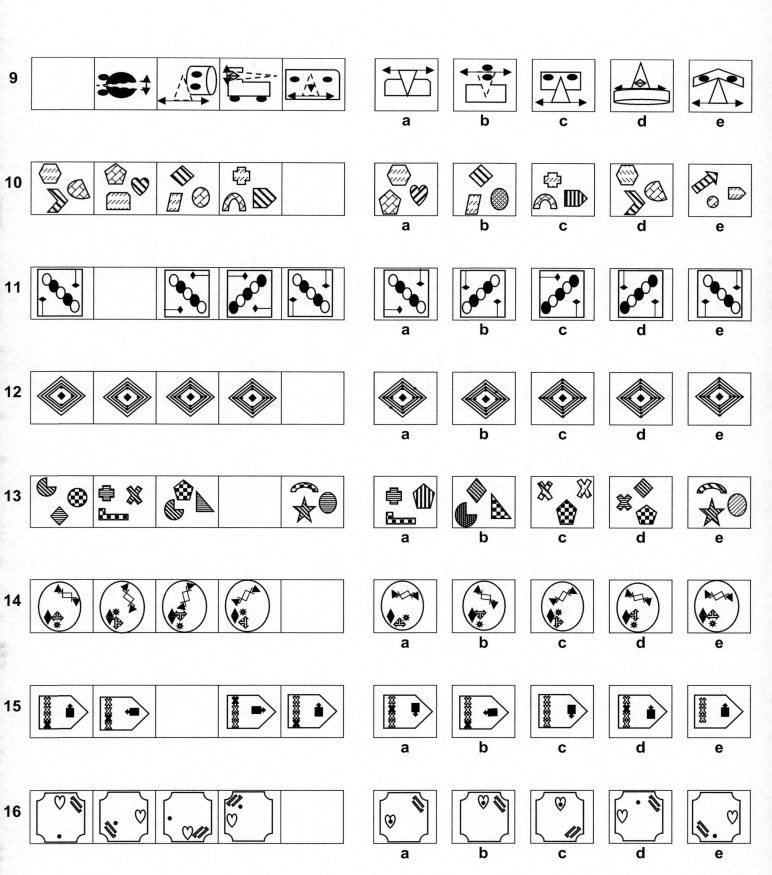

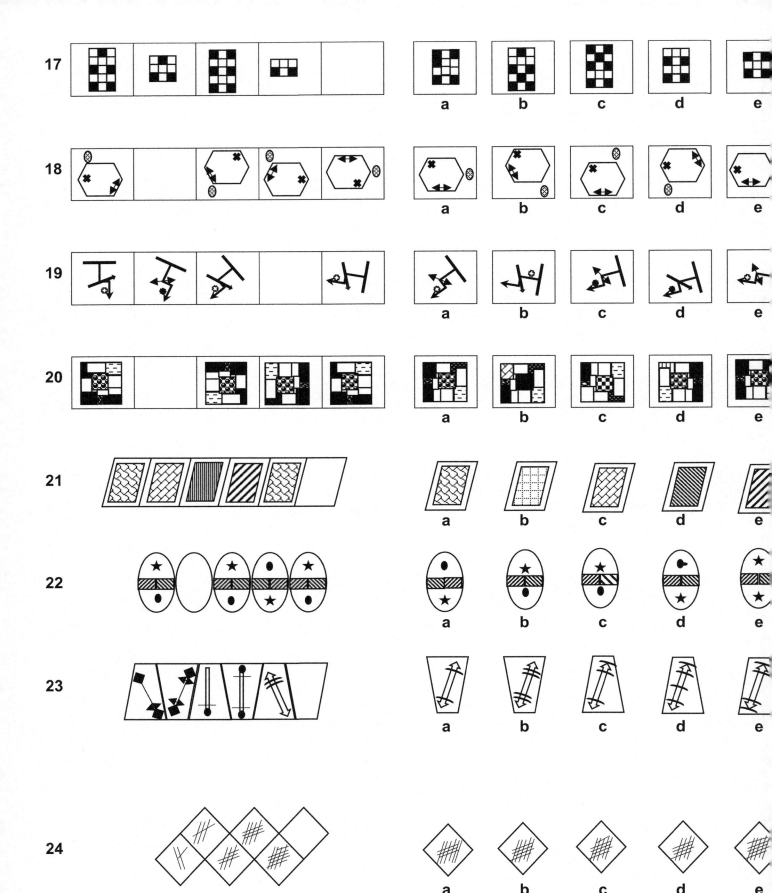

25

 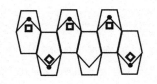

a   b   c   d   e

26

a   b   c   d   e

In Matrices questions, you are given a grid of either four or nine squares. In each type, you have to develop the common rules of how a shape changes throughout the grid. Matrices build on the NVR techniques that you learnt with both Analogy and Sequences. It is significant to review those sections before tackling NVR Matrices.

Here's some patterns that might occur in the matrix grid. You should immediately try and spot either an analogy or a sequence that might be occurring in these directions:

Clockwise or anticlockwise

Snaking right one row and left the next row

Snaking down one column and up the next

Diagonally

Down or up each row

Across each row

Example of a 4 by 4 Grid using **analogy.**

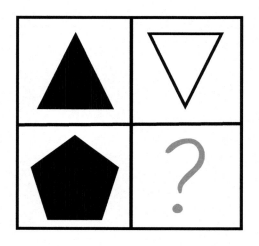

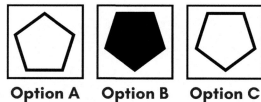

Option A   Option B   Option C

Here the triangle changes shading from black to white and rotates by 180°. So, the answer must have white shading, which rules out Option B and also must be pointing downward, which also eliminates Option A.
Option C is the correct answer!

43

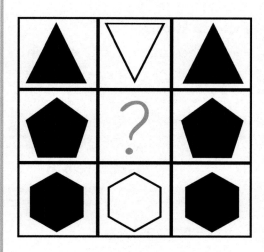

Option A **Option B** **Option C** **Option D**

This is a horizontal series. This middle shape has to be a pentagon, which rules out option D. It also needs to be shaded white, which rules out option A and C. This leaves us with option B, which follows all the rule that the middle shape shape has to be rotated by 180°.

<u>Option B is the correct answer!</u>

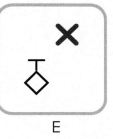 Example Question

Which option correctly completes the given matrix?

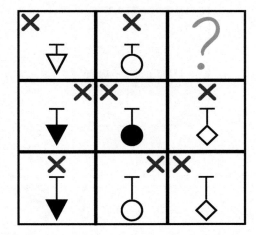

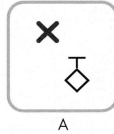 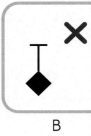 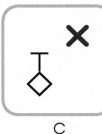 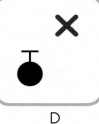 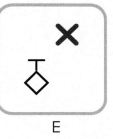

A   B   C   D   E

 Identify **key attributes** among the images in the matrix.

- **Shape:** Each image has either a **triangle**, a **circle** or a **diamond**.
- **Size:** The vertical lines are either **short, medium** or **long**.
- **Colour:** The shapes are either **white** or **black**.
- **Position:** The '**x**' is either placed on the left, center or right side of the box.

2 Work out how the attributes are organized in a sequence.

3

Shape	Line Length

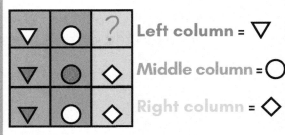 **Left column** = ▽
Middle column = ○
Right column = ◇

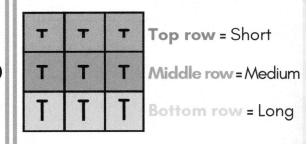 **Top row** = Short
Middle row = Medium
Bottom row = Long

The **X** is on the...
Left
Middle
Right

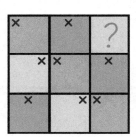

Each row uses the following three **X** positions: **left, middle, right.** These don't seem to be following any specific sequence, but we know that they have to be in each of those positions, so we can figure out which position is missing in the top row.

 We can rule out option B and C because there **line length** are too long. The X in option A is in the wrong position. We can also rule out option D as it has a wrong shape.

 Option E is the correct answer!

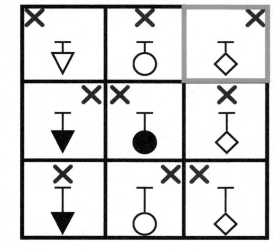

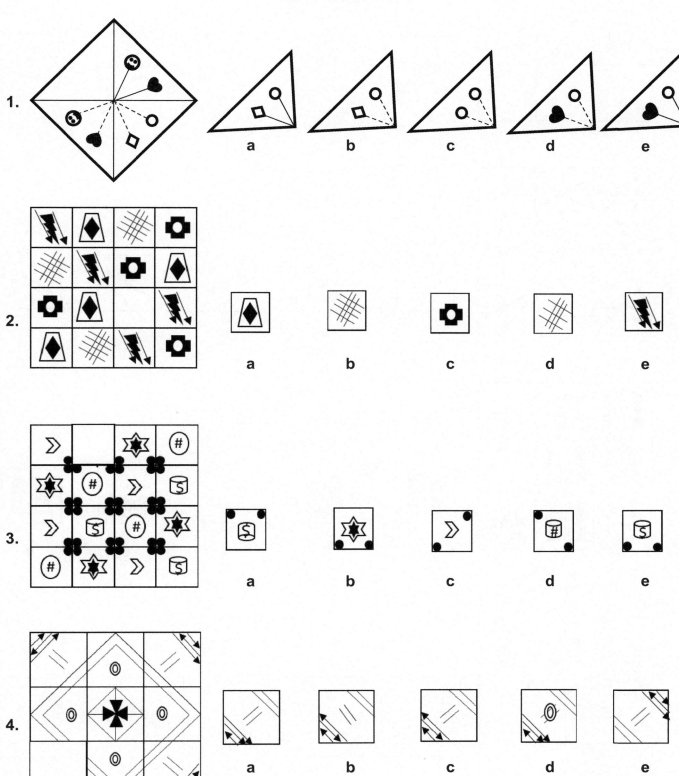

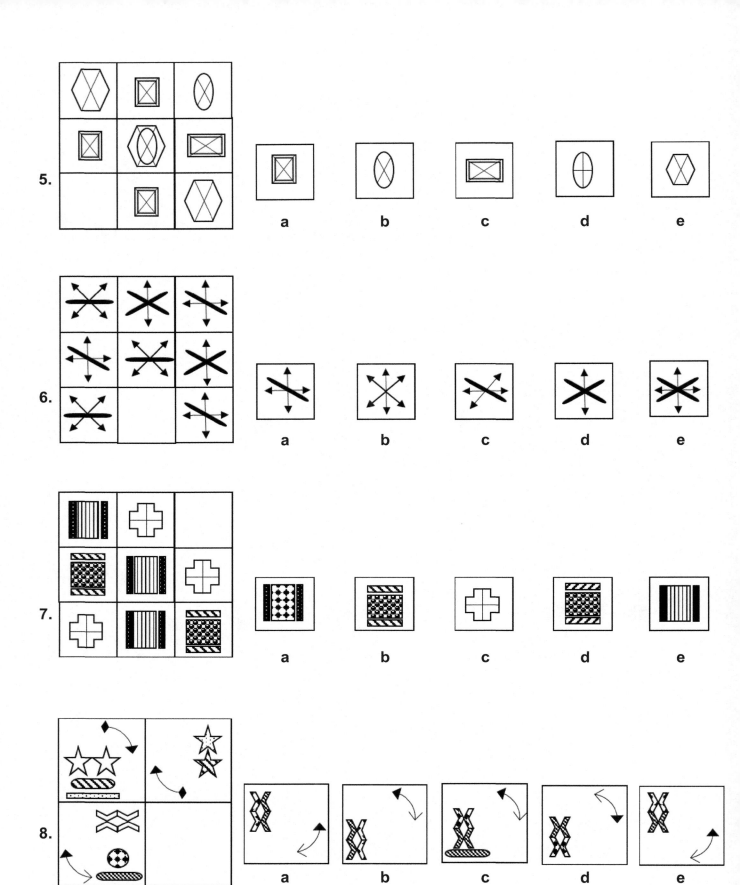

5.

6.

7.

8.

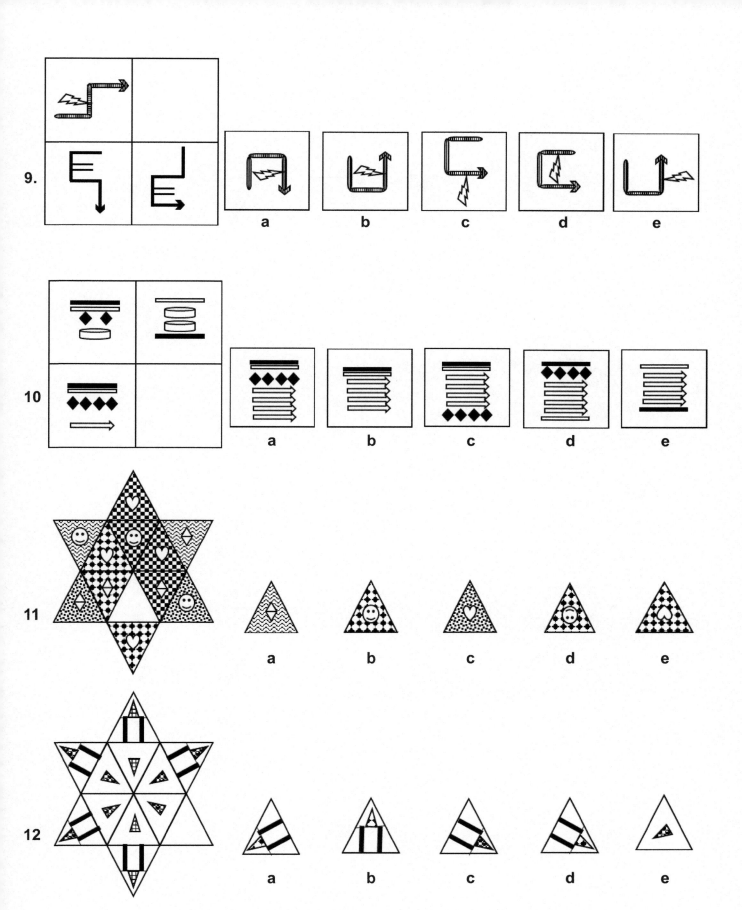

9.

10.

11.

12.

48

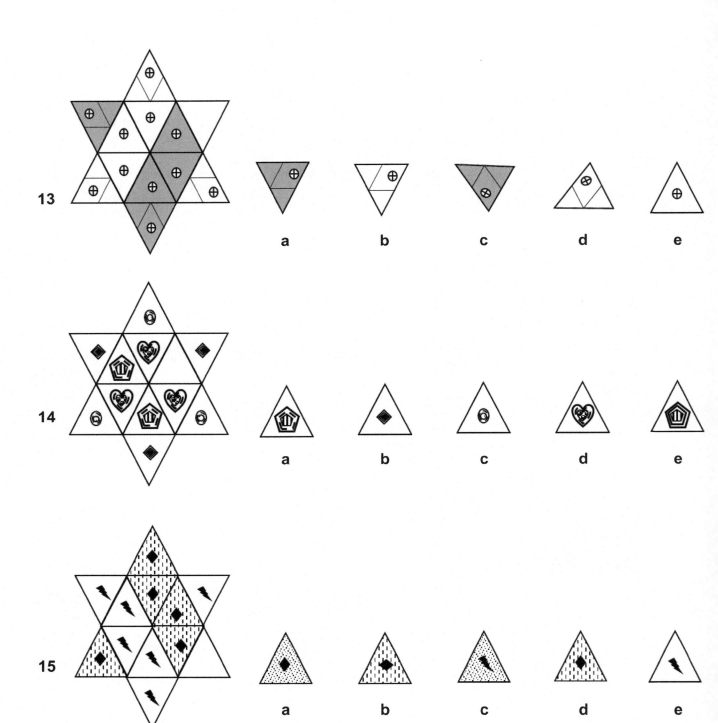

13
a b c d e

14
a b c d e

15
a b c d e

In Code questions, you are given a picture that is connected with two or three letters. Each letter represents one or more of the NVR properties.

Never Sneak Snacks To A Crowded Picnic!

| Number | Size | Shape | Total | Angle | Colour | Pattern |

M.O.P.S. - Movement Orientation, Placement, Symmetry

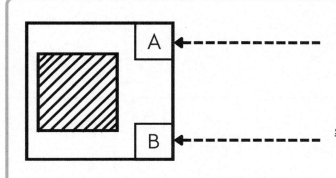

For example, Letters in this <u>position could stand for shape</u>, which will then mean the Letter itself stands for the <u>type of shape</u> (e.g. square)

While a Letter in this <u>position could stand for shading</u>, which means the Letter itself stands for the <u>type of shading</u> (e.g. diagonal lines)

Approach

To actually work out what property a letter stands for, and what type of property it is – you have to compare it with other shapes. You should identify the **duplicate** letters and **find out** what they have in **common** .

Shape 1

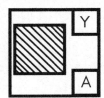

Shape 2

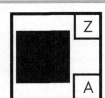

Shape 3

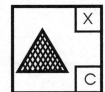

Shape 4

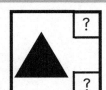

Test Shape

1 Start with the top letters: Shape 1 and 2 both have letter Z. The common property they have is the shading (black). This means the top letter position is about shading. <u>Z means black</u>, Y means diagonal and X means crisscross shading.

2 Next, in the bottom letters: Shape 2 and 3 both have letter A, which shares a common property of shape (square). This means the bottom letter is about shape. A means square, <u>C means triangle</u> and B means pentagon.

3 Start with the top letters: Shape 1 and 2 both have letter Z. The common property they have is the shading (black). This means the top letter position is about shading. <u>Z means black,</u> Y means diagonal and X means crisscross shading.

Look out: Sometimes the same letters can be used in different positions of the code. Which means that they will refer to different attributes! For example: A in the top position is not the same as A in the bottom position!

Example Question

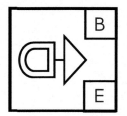 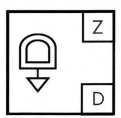 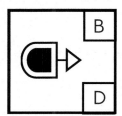 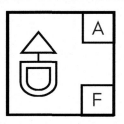 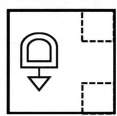

1 Look at the images with the **same letters** and see what properties they share.

- **Top letter**: Where images share the same top letter, the shapes are **oriented** the same way.
- **Bottom letter**: Where images share the same bottom letter, the triangle is the same size.

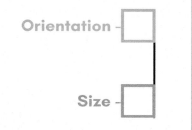

Colour is an **irrelevant property.** We know this because only one of the images have a black shape, despite it having the same letter as the other images.

2 Work out what each top letter – A, B, C – and what each bottom letter – D, E, F – means.

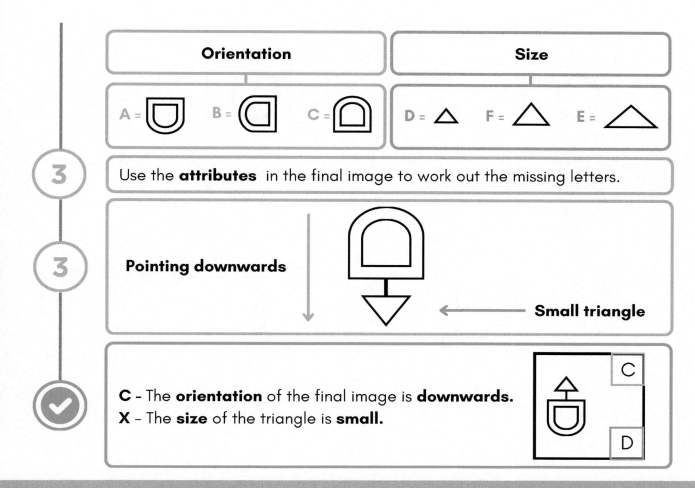

Orientation			Size		
A =	B =	C =	D =	F =	E =

3 Use the **attributes** in the final image to work out the missing letters.

3

Pointing downwards

Small triangle

✓ **C** - The **orientation** of the final image is **downwards.**
X - The **size** of the triangle is **small.**

🏆 Top Tips

 The same letter may be used in **more than one position** in the code! If the same letter is in a different position, it will represent a **different attribute.**

 Compare the images that **share the same letter** and imagine filtering out the differences. The similarities that are left are connected to the letter code.

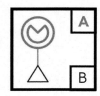 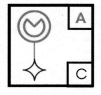 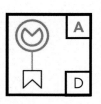

 Don't forget! Focus on 1 letter code at a time and compare the images that share them.

 Look out for **red herrings!** These are irrelevant attributes that will be shared between images to confuse you.

NVR Codes

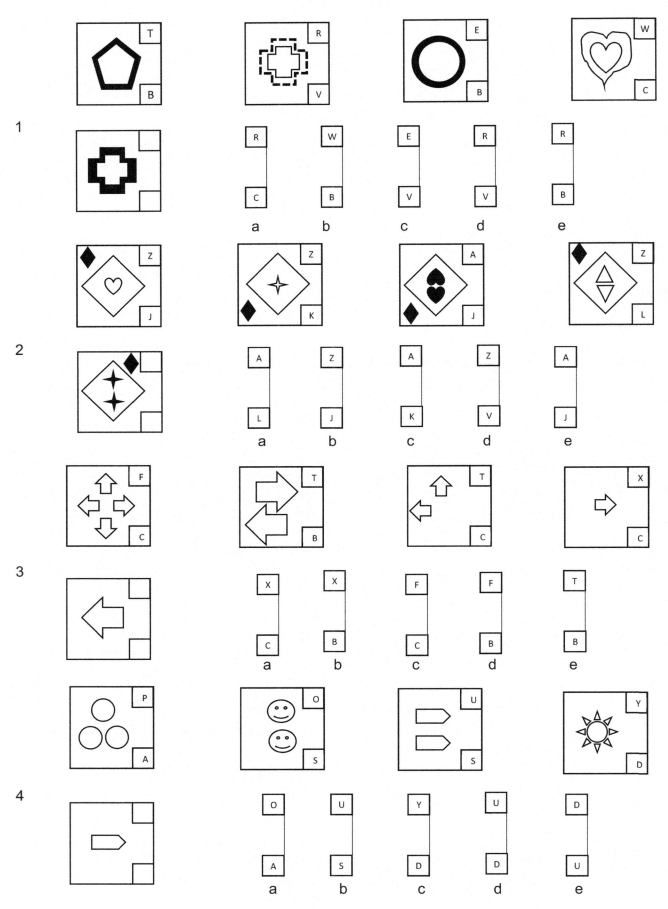

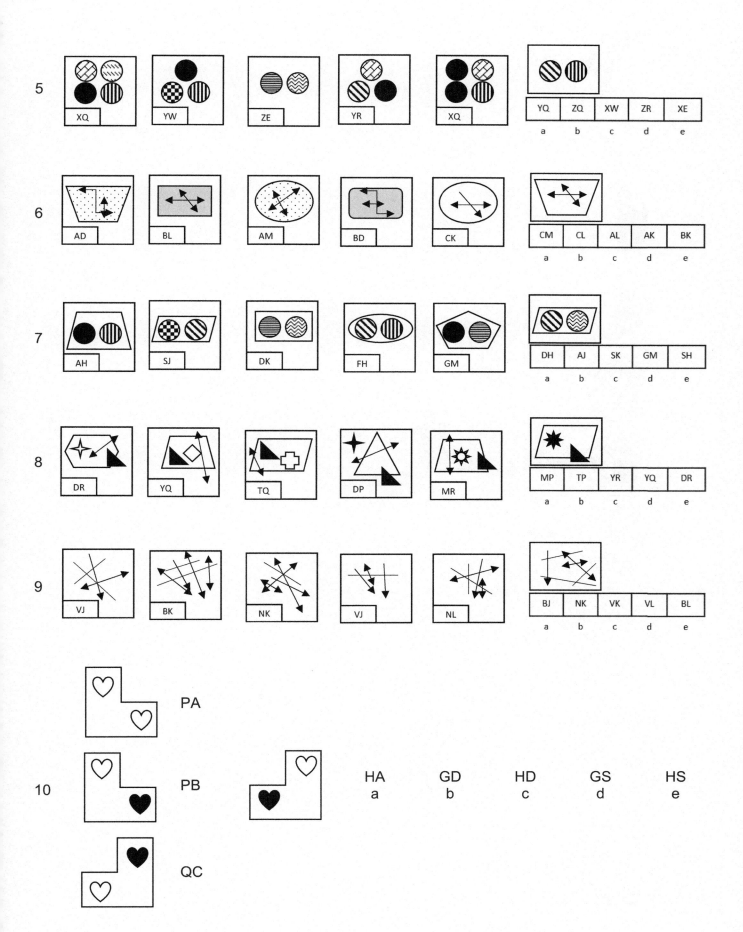

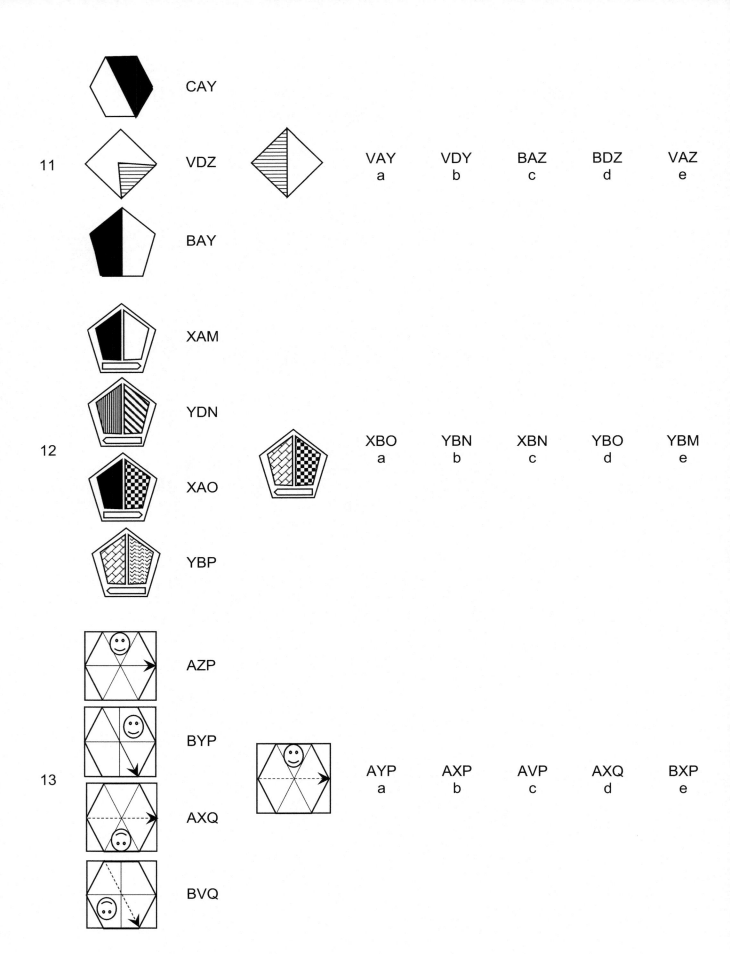

CAY

11   VDZ   VAY   VDY   BAZ   BDZ   VAZ
              a   b   c   d   e

BAY

XAM

YDN

12   XAO   XBO   YBN   XBN   YBO   YBM
              a   b   c   d   e

YBP

AZP

BYP

13   AXQ   AYP   AXP   AVP   AXQ   BXP
              a   b   c   d   e

BVQ

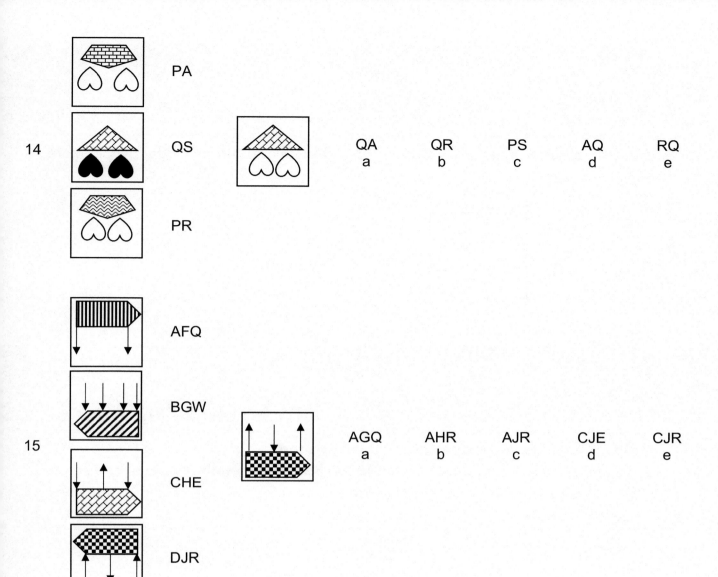

14

PA

QS

PR

QA	QR	PS	AQ	RQ
a	b	c	d	e

15

AFQ

BGW

CHE

DJR

AGQ	AHR	AJR	CJE	CJR
a	b	c	d	e

In hidden shapes questions, you have to find an image that is hidden within more complex shape.

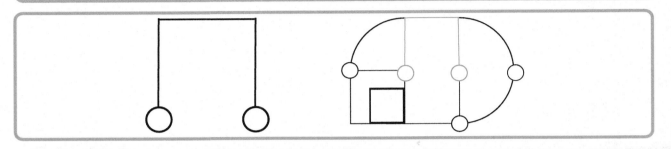

Approach

1. Check if the hidden shape has not been **rotated.**
2. Isolate and Eliminate: **Break the hidden shape into smaller pieces** and see if any of these match your set of larger range of hiding places. Eliminate any answers if possible.

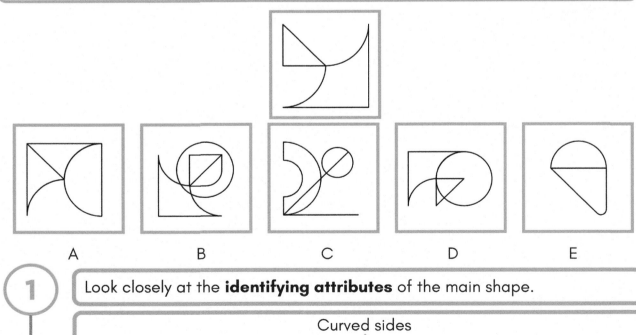

A   B   C   D   E

1   Look closely at the **identifying attributes** of the main shape.

Curved sides

Right-angled triangle ------->

Connected at this corner

Right-angled arrow

2 Rule out the options that are **obviously** incorrect.

We can rule out...
- Option **C** and **E** because they don't have anything that resembles the main shape

3 We can rule out **D** because it do not have a **right-angled triangle.**

D is a **red herring!** It looks very similar to the main shape, but we can rule it out because the right-angled triangle is connected to the arrow by the **wrong corner.**

Option C is the correct answer! It's the only option that contains the main shape – it has been rotated 90° clockwise.

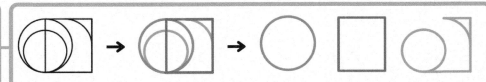

 Top Tips

Look out for well-hidden shapes!
Shapes might be hidden in such a way that they form part of larger shape. Imagine separating out each line or curve until you find the hidden shape!

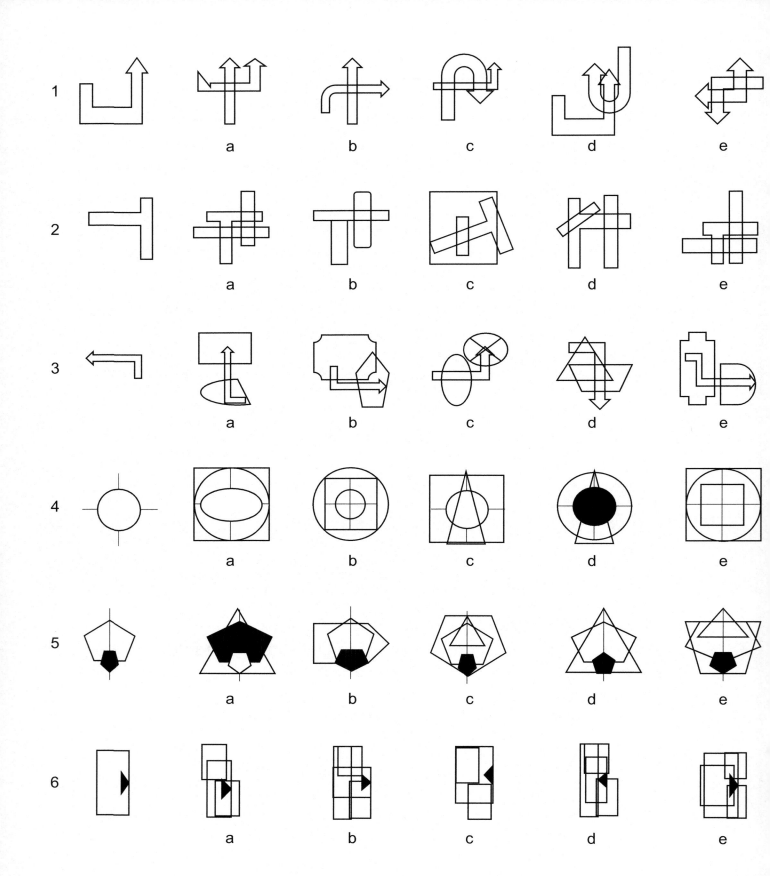

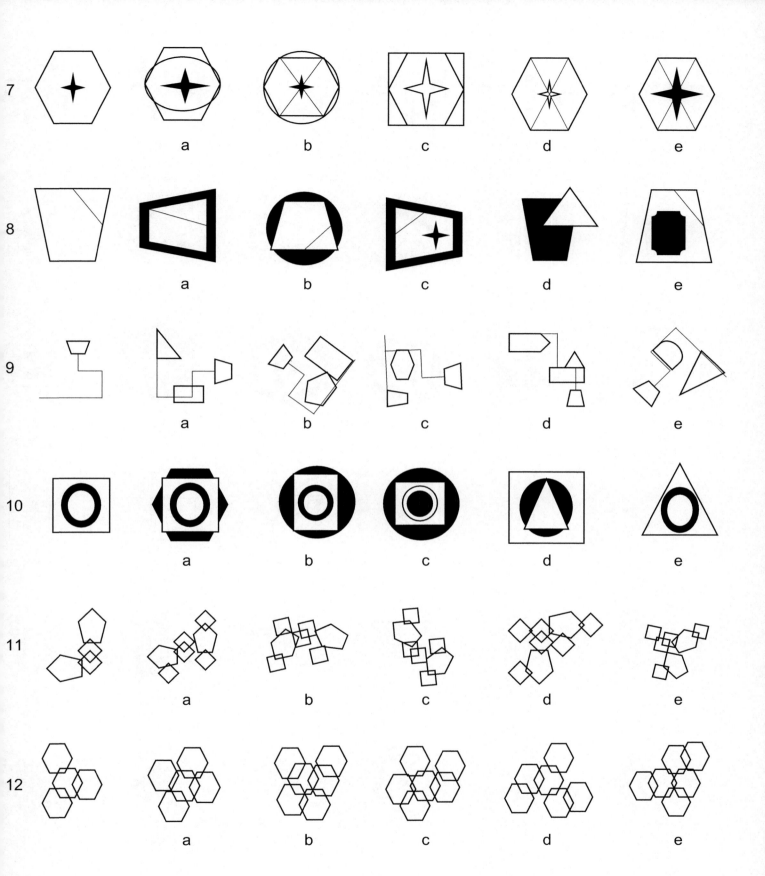

7

a b c d e

8

a b c d e

9

a b c d e

10

a b c d e

11

a b c d e

12

a b c d e

60

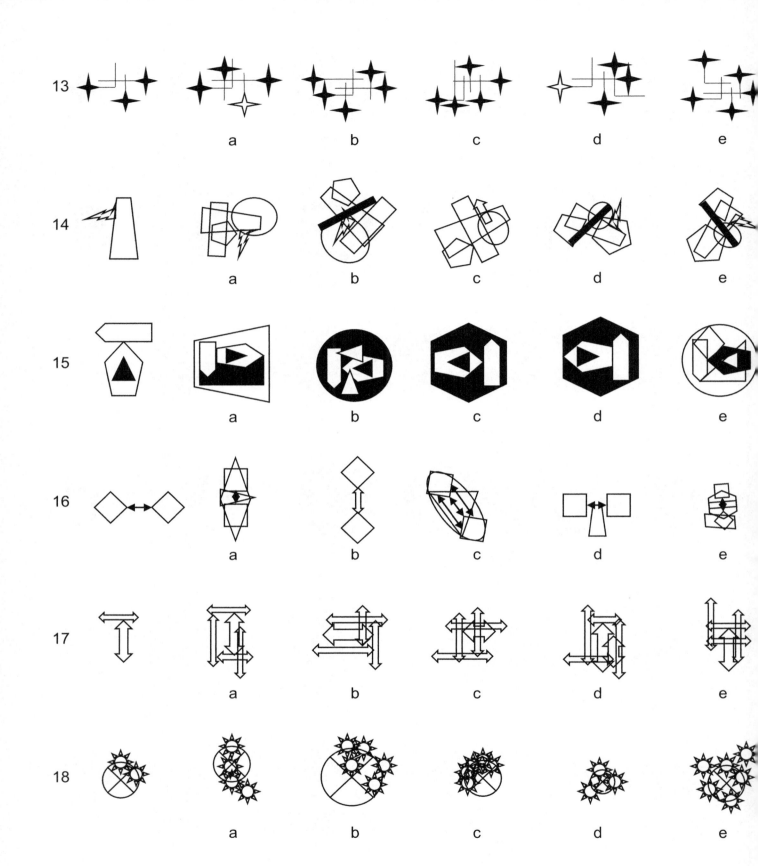

13 a b c d e

14 a b c d e

15 a b c d e

16 a b c d e

17 a b c d e

18 a b c d e

19

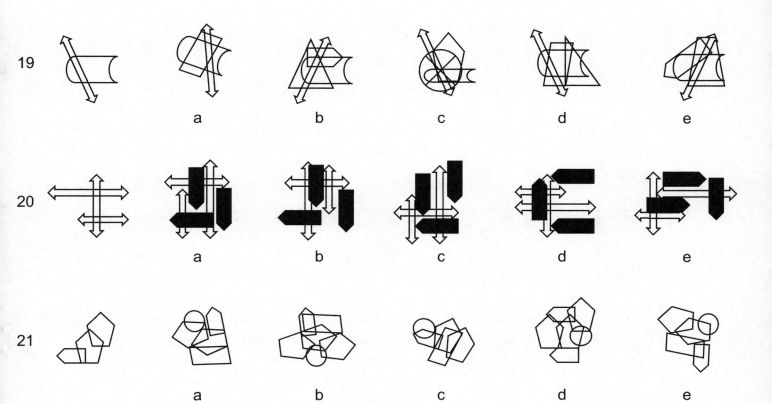

               a   b   c   d   e

20

               a   b   c   d   e

21

               a   b   c   d   e

NVR TYPE 10: COMBINING SHAPES

In combining shapes questions, you are given two shapes. These shapes have been combined into a new shape that you have to identify from a range of given shapes.

 Approach

1 Look closely at each shapes you need to combine and identify the key NVR properties of each shape that must be present in the answer.

In this given example, the main **identifying attributes** we need to look out for are:
- pattern
- shape
- colour

2 Focus on the **first shape** and then rule out any options that do not contain this shape.

1st Shape

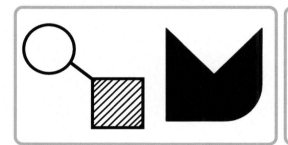

3 Repeat this process for the **second shapes.**

You should be left with **one option** that is an **exact combination** of the two given shapes!

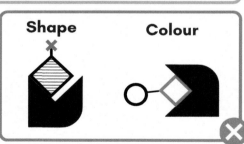

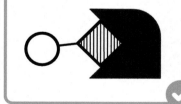

 Don't forget! Correct answer may have been rotated, but its proportion will always remain the same!

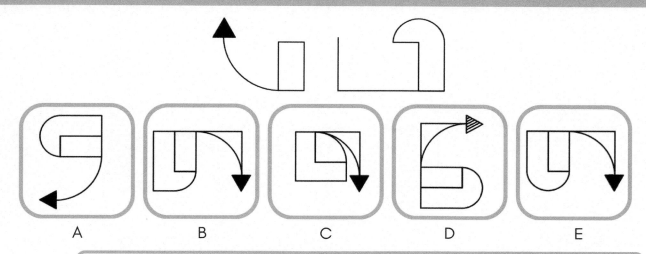

A   B   C   D   E

1 Look for the NVR Properties in each shape.
- **First Shape:** The first shape is a black curved arrow attached to a white rectangle at the bottom-left corner.
- **Second Shape:** The second shape is made of right angled line attached to a white shape made up of a rectangle and a semicircle on top.

2 Eliminate any options that do not contain the first shape.

1st Shape

We can eliminate...
- **Option D** because the triangle is lined, not black.
- **Option C** because rectangle is not present.

3 Eliminate any options that don't contain the **second shape.**

2nd Shape

We can eliminate...
- **Option A** because the right angled line that sticks out of the 2nd shape is missing.

Option D is a **red herring!** It looks like the correct answer, but if you carefully look at it, we can seen the dome part of the rectangular shape is different: it has a right angled corner.

Option E is the correct answer!

Combination Shapes

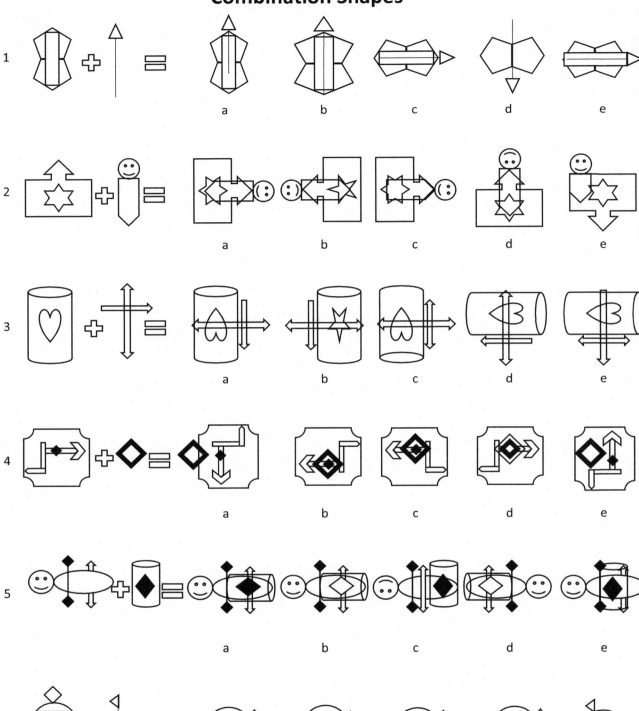

In folding and hole punching questions, you may be asked to fold a shape along a line as below:

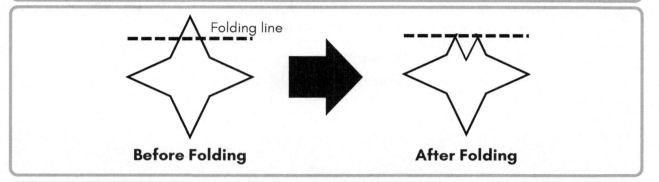

Folding line

Before Folding   **After Folding**

Or you may be asked to fold the shape multiple times and then also hole punch it and unfold it:

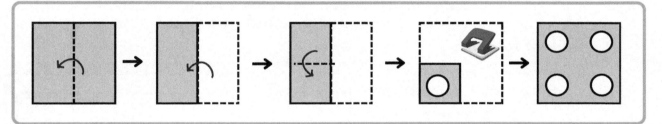

 Top Tips

 The folding line acts like a **line of reflection.** So, you must apply your NVR reflection techniques here. The aftermath fold will be a mirror image with a **creased up fold line.**

 Make sure you fold at the right place; the aftermath fold will likely overlap the original shape.

 Approach

① Look at how the paper has been folded and **count the number of layers.**

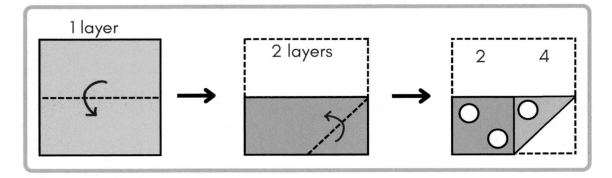

1 layer → 2 layers → 2   4

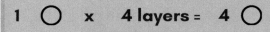

② **Calculate the total number of holes** in the unfolded paper by multiplying the number of shapes by the number of layers they were cut out from.

2 ○ x 2 layers = 4 ○   1 ○ x 4 layers = 4 ○

⊗ **Rule out** any options that have the **incorrect number of holes!**

③ Imagine **unfolding** the paper **one fold at a time,** starting with the **last fold** and working backwards.

Every fold acts as a line of symmetry, so the shapes will be reflected across the folds!

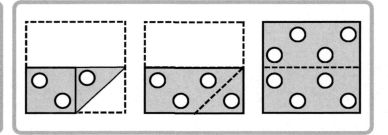

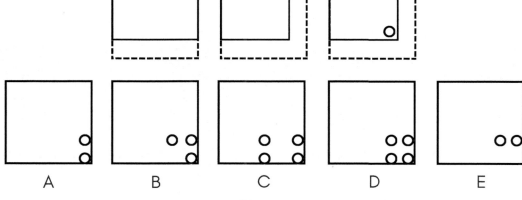

Example Question

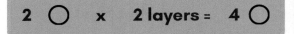

A   B   C   D   E

1 Check how many layers are there in the folded paper.

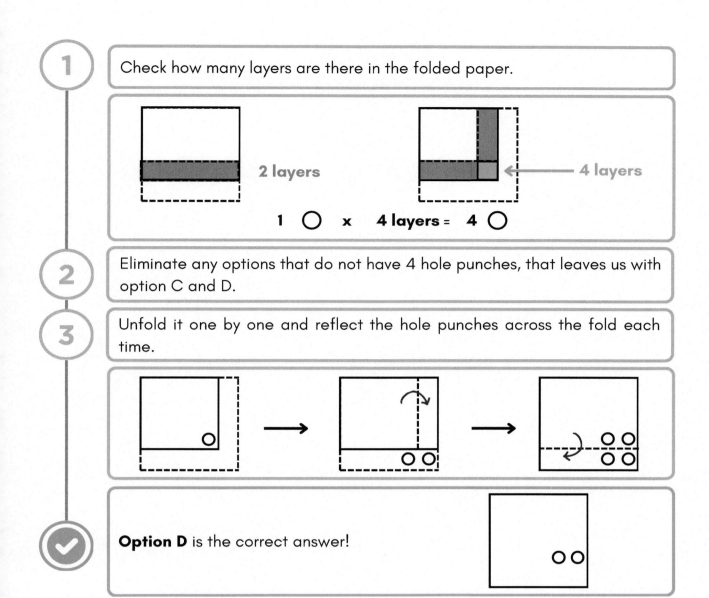

2 layers

4 layers

1 ○ x **4 layers** = 4 ○

2 Eliminate any options that do not have 4 hole punches, that leaves us with option C and D.

3 Unfold it one by one and reflect the hole punches across the fold each time.

Option D is the correct answer!

Top Tips

Don't forget! Imagine each fold in the paper as a **line of symmetry**. How would the shapes look like if they were reflected across a horizontal vertical or diagonal fold?

Pay attention to the distance between a shape and a fold. This will help you figure out where it should be positioned on the unfolded paper.

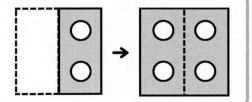

NVR Spatial Reasoning : Folding

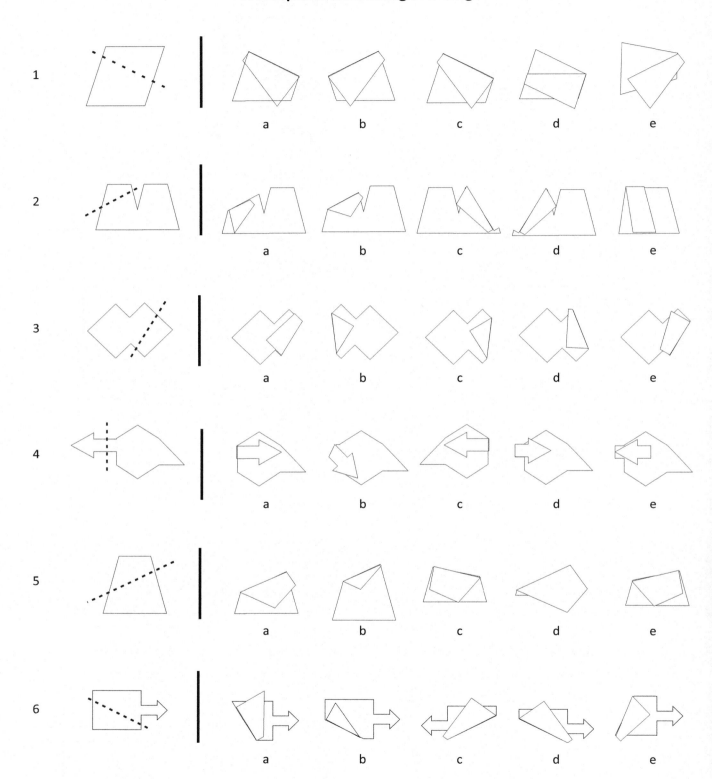

Fold, hole-punch and then unfold : what do you see now?

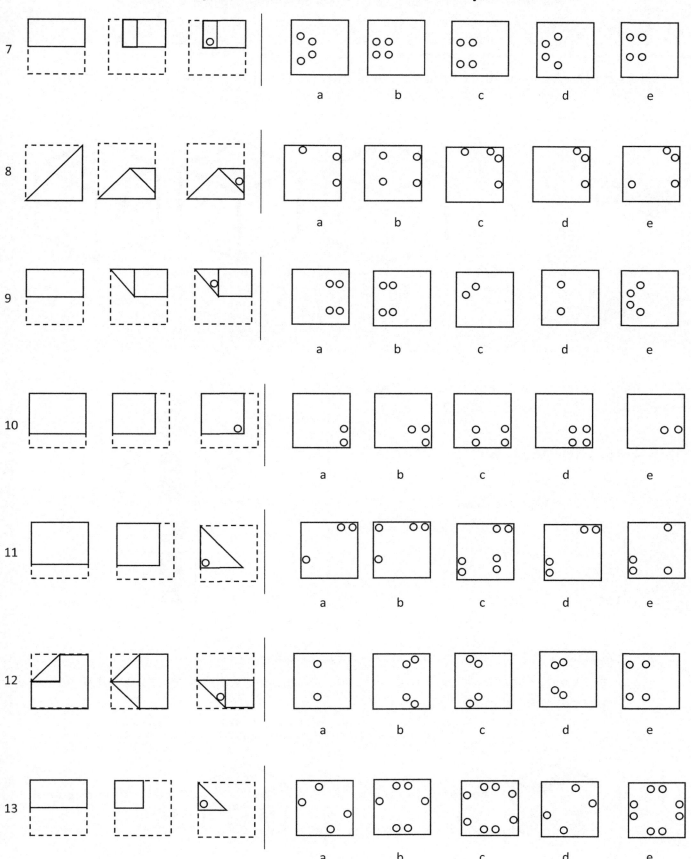

In Nets and Cubes questions, you will be shown a 2D net and asked to work out what it would look like when it is folded up into a cube.

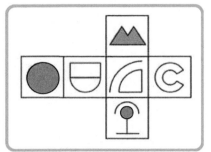

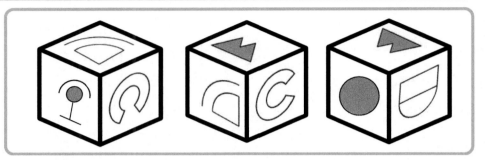

Approach

We recommend following four steps (Simplified by the mnemonic MORE)

M check for **Match**

O check for **Opposites**

R check for **Rotation**

E check for **Edge**

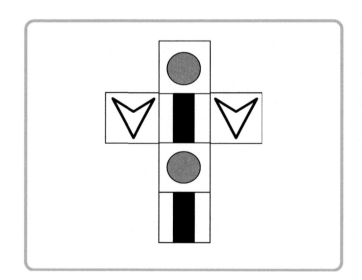

1 **Match:** Check that patterns on the net match with patterns on the cube – otherwise eliminate.

 The arrow shape is the wrong colour.

 The X shape **does not exist**.

Opposite: The opposite faces on a cube will always be a space away on the net. (If not, then eliminate from your choices.)

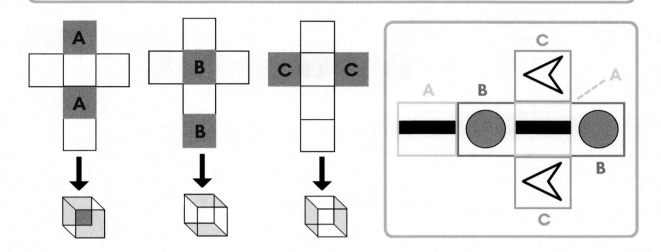

Breaking the opposites rule

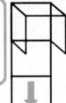

3

Rotation: Beware of rotation – the images on a face may appear to rotate as they are folded upwards or sideways.

Arrow originally pointing down, but points up when folded.

Breaking the orientation rule

 The triangle should not point towards the line.

 The 'lever' should point towards the circle!

Edges: Check that the edges match.

Here the arrows are pointing to the white circle

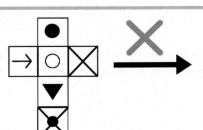

Arrow is not pointing to the white circle – so eliminate

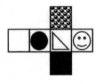

a   b   c   d   e

1 First let's **match** our options to the original, and cancel out any options that have mismatched shapes.

We can't eliminate any options because they all only include shapes from the original net.

2 Now let's check for **opposites** :

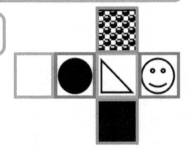

We can eliminate
- **B** because the smiley face should be opposite the black circle
- **D** because the black side should be opposite the dotted side

3 Now let's check the **rotation and edges** of the shapes

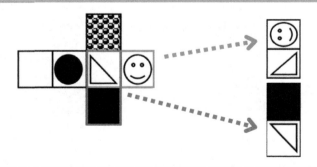

We can eliminate
- **C** because the smiley face should be rotated sideways, as shown above, if the tip of the triangle is on it's edge.
- **E** because the flat base of the triangle should face the black side, as shown above.

 So, the correct answer is **A:**

a

There are three pairs of opposite squares on every net. The opposite faces in the nets below are indicated by the **same colours and numbers!**

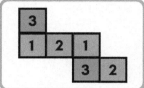 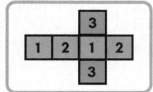 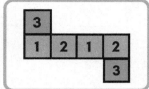 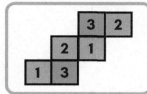

Look for **identifying features** on a shape, such as points or arrowheads, to figure out which faces it's pointing towards.

Sometimes it can help to visualise the folding process ...

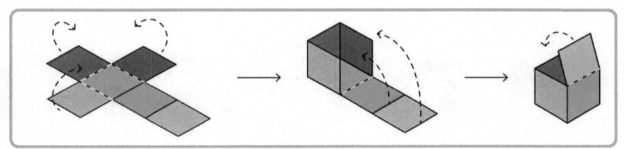

74

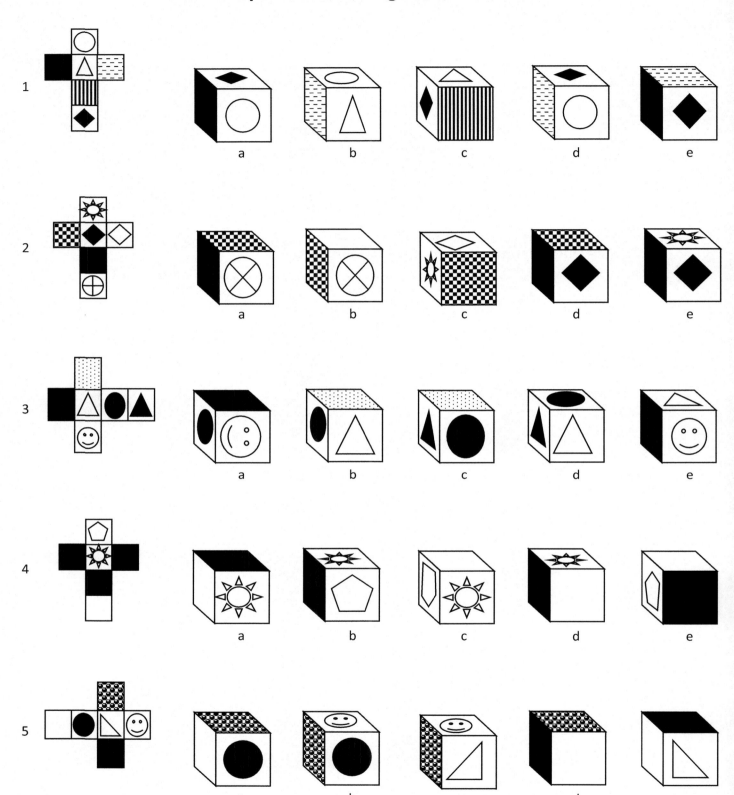

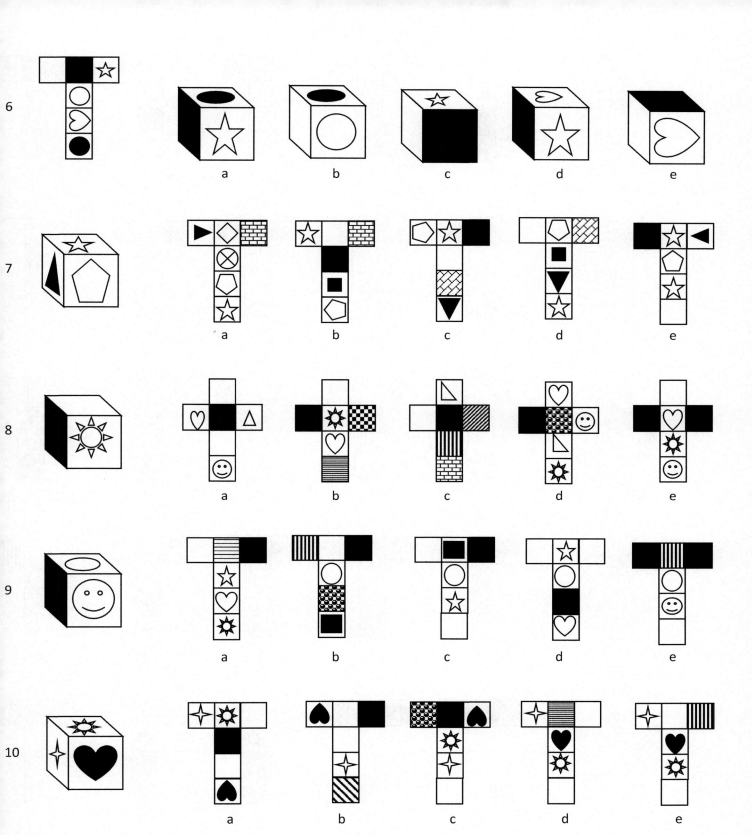

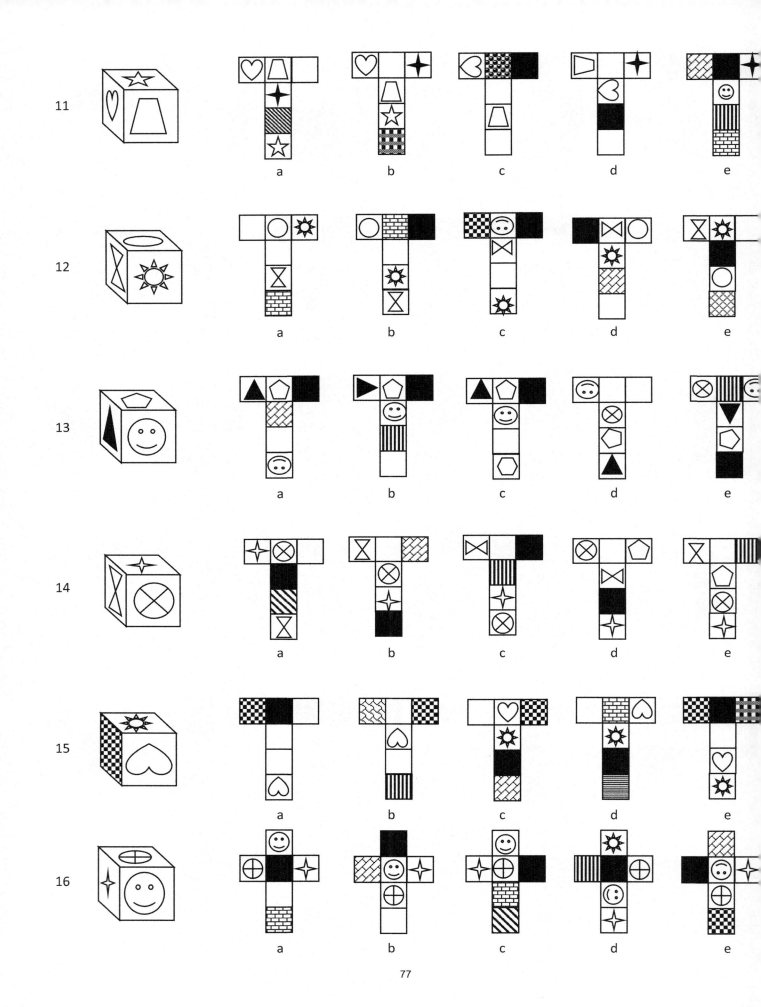

In the **NVR 2D View of 3D Shapes questions**, you are given a 3D Shape, and are then asked to imagine what the 2D view would look like from a particular viewpoint. An example is shown below:

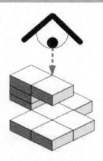

Remember when viewing:
- You only see 2D squares.
- Some of the squares will be hidden from the view by the blocks above it.
- Finally, you should see if there are rows of the blocks. This will need to be reflected in your view.

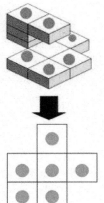

One way to deal with these type of questions is colour (like we have done here with circles) the top of the blocks, which is what will be seen from above. It will also make it easier to identify blocks that are hidden from the view.

This is what you are likely to see from above. Don't forget to isolate and eliminate your answer options to help you rule out wrong answers if the blocks have a complex layout.

Don't worry about the **height** of the 3D shape, just focus on the **top blocks** - these are the only blocks you can see when looking at the shape from above!

 1

Look at the **dimensions** of the 3D shape.

- How many blocks **wide** is it?
- How many blocks **long** is it?
- Can you rule out any answer options?

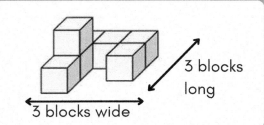

3 blocks long

3 blocks wide

2 Start by looking at the **top blocks** in the **first row**. Compare the number and position of any **top blocks** with each answer option.

Are there ....
- the correct **number** of blocks?
- **top blocks** in the correct positions?
- any extra or missing **gaps?**

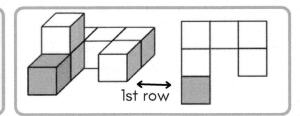

1st row

3 Work through **each row of blocks**, asking the same questions, until you have worked through every row and ruled out all the incorrect answer options.

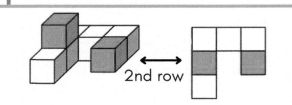

2nd row

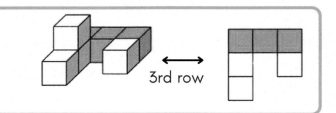

3rd row

Top Tips

Look out for the **overhanging blocks** (blocks that stick out over a gap with nothing underneath them) and **obscured blocks** (blocks that you can only see part of) – they may be used to confuse you!

Obscured Blocks	**Overhanging Blocks**
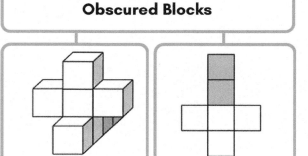	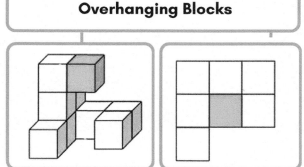

2D View from the Left

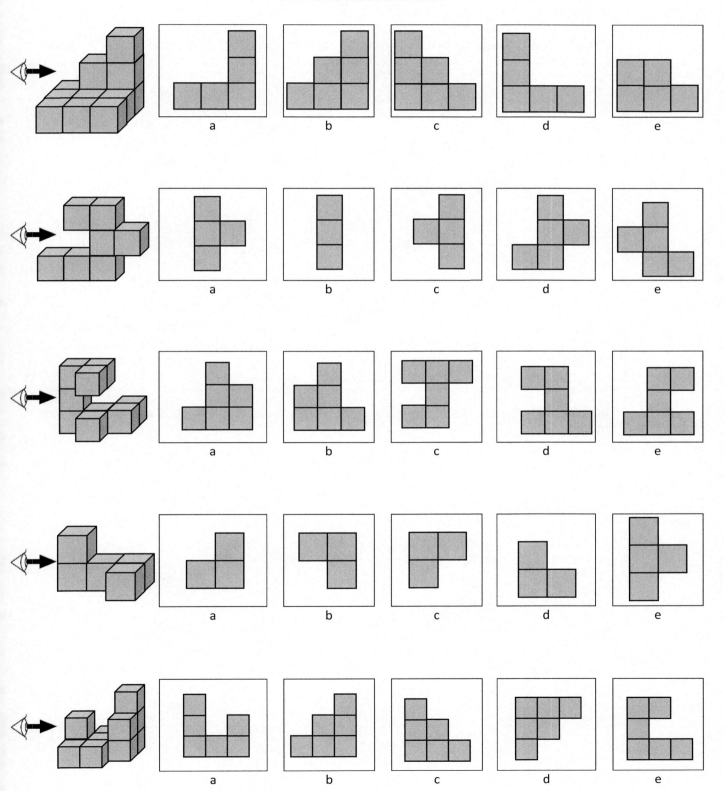

3D Building Blocks:

In the NVR 3D Building Blocks, you are given a 3D shape and you have to identify from a choice of building blocks which of them need to be put together to make the given 3D shape.

For instance, the shape below can be assembled from the blocks on the right:

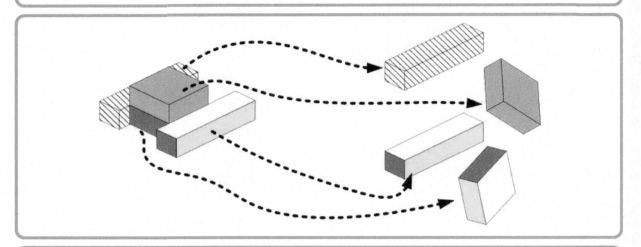

Remember, although the building blocks can be rotated, they are essentially the same shape, size, shade and number as the original assembled building block.

 Eliminate any shape in which the number, type or size of the blocks do not match.

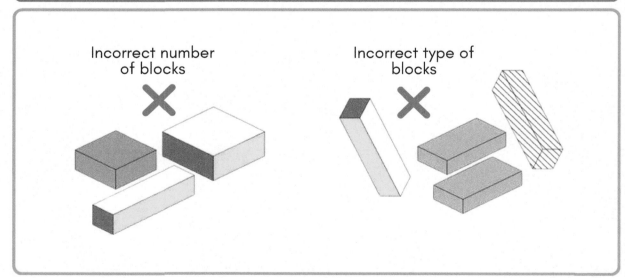

Incorrect number of blocks

Incorrect type of blocks

NVR Spatial Reasoning : 3D Building Blocks

Which blocks on the right can be put together to make the test shape

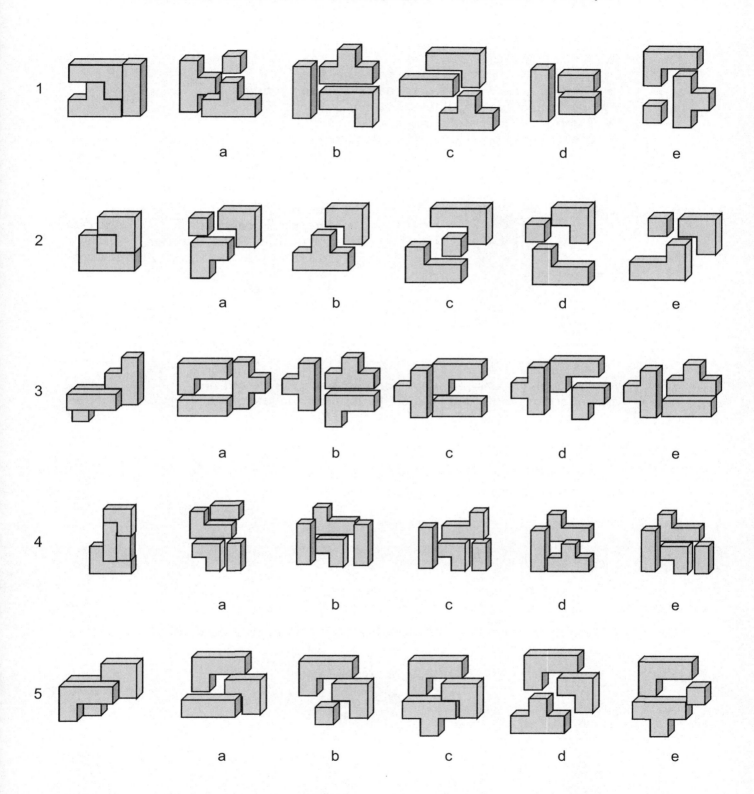

1   a   b   c   d   e

2   a   b   c   d   e

3   a   b   c   d   e

4   a   b   c   d   e

5   a   b   c   d   e

Rotating 3D Shapes:

Look closely at the **identifying features** of the main 3D shape.

Think about NAPS!
- **Number:** How many blocks are there in total?
- **Angles:** Are any blocks perpendicular to each other? Are any blocks parallel to each other?
- **Position:** Which blocks are next to each other?
- **Size:** How long, tall or wide is each block?

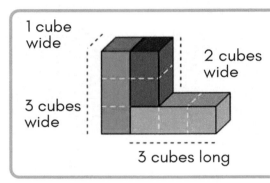

1 cube wide

2 cubes wide

3 cubes wide

3 cubes long

- **Number:** There are three blocks.
- **Angles & Position:** The upright blocks are parallel to each other, and the green and yellow blocks are perpendicular to each other.
- **Size:** See diagram.

Work through the answer options **one by one** and **rule out** any answer options that do not match the features you identified.

Number

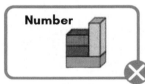

You should be left with one option that shows an exact **rotation** of the original 3D shape!

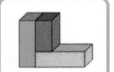

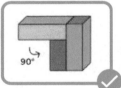

90°

Example Question

Which of the options below is a rotation of this 3D Shape?

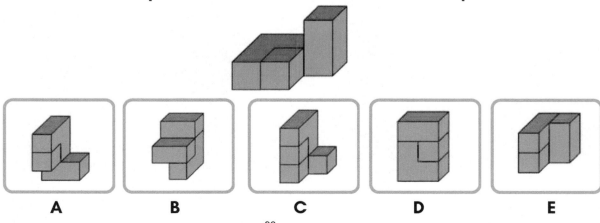

A   B   C   D   E

1 Identify the main **features of the 3D shape.**

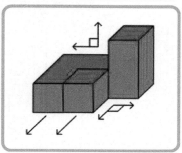

- **Number:** There are three blocks in total.
- **Angle:** See diagram.
- **Position:** The cube is tucked inside the L-shape. The cuboid extends from one face of the L-shape.
- **Size:** There is a 2x1 cuboid (block 1), a 2x2 L-shape (block 2) and a 1x1 cube (block 3).

Block 1	**Block 2**	**Block 3**
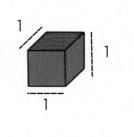	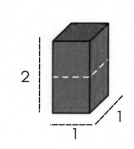	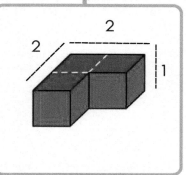

2 Use **NAPS** – number, angle, position, size – to **rule out answer options.**

We can rule out....
- **A** because block 3 has been replaced by a longer block.
- **C** because there are **four** blocks instead of three.
- **E** because block 1 is **positioned incorrectly.**

D is a **red herring!** It looks like it could be the correct answer, but if you look closely you can see that block 1 has not been rotated!

B is the correct answer! It is a 90° clockwise rotation of the 3D shape.

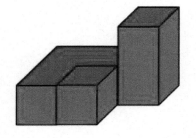 90°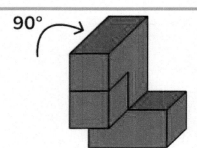

Work out which 3D figure (a, b, c, d, e or f) has been rotated to make the new 3D figure

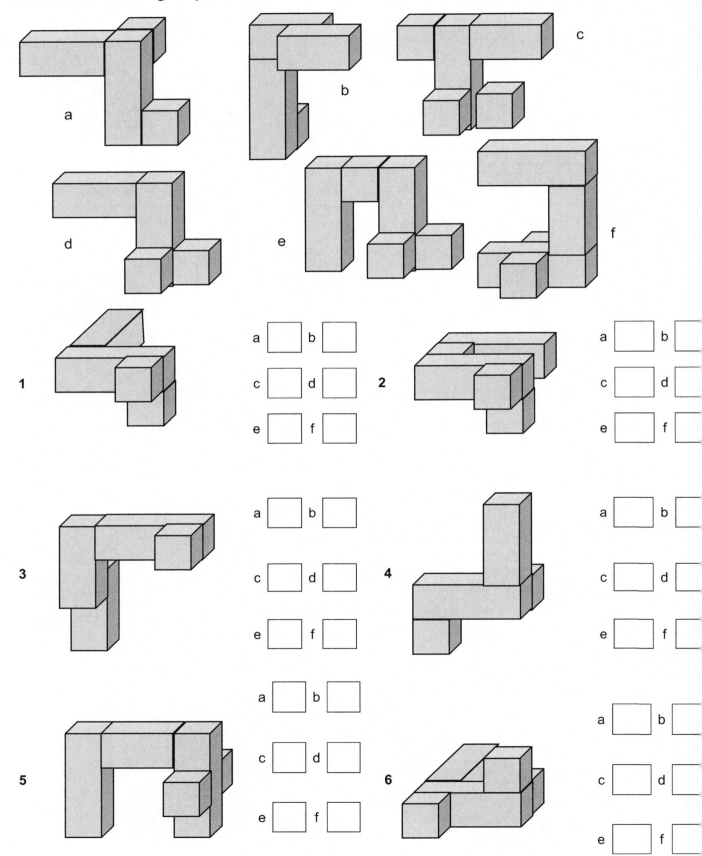

a

b

c

d

e

f

1

a ☐ b ☐

c ☐ d ☐

e ☐ f ☐

2

a ☐ b ☐

c ☐ d ☐

e ☐ f ☐

3

a ☐ b ☐

c ☐ d ☐

e ☐ f ☐

4

a ☐ b ☐

c ☐ d ☐

e ☐ f ☐

5

a ☐ b ☐

c ☐ d ☐

e ☐ f ☐

6

a ☐ b ☐

c ☐ d ☐

e ☐ f ☐

Answer Key
Non Verbal Reasoning Question Types

Odd One Out:	Similarites:	Reflections:	Rotations:	Analogy:	Series:	Matrices:
1. c	1.c	1 d	1 b	1 d	1. b	1.a
2. b	2.c	2 b	2 d	2 c	2. d	2.b
3. c	3.e	3 e	3 c	3 a	3. d	3.e
4. c	4.e	4 a	4 c	4 c	4. a	4.c
5. d	5.c	5 c	5 e	5 e	5. c	5.b
6. a	6.e	6 d	6 a	6 b	6. d	6.d
7. d	7.b	7 c	7 d	7 a	7. b	7.b
8. d	8.a	8 e	8 d	8 e	8. c	8.d
9. b	9.e	9 b	9 b	9 c	9. b	9.b
10. c	10.d	10 a	10 e	10 d	10. e	10.e
11. d	11.b	11 c		11 c	11. d	11.b
12. d	12.b	12 d		12 e	12. e	12.c
13. b	13.e	13 d		13 e	13. d	13.a
14. a	14.d	14 c		14 d	14. e	14.a
15. a	15.c	15 c		15 b	15. a	15.d
16. b	16.b	16 e		16 c	16. b	
17. c	17.b	17 b		17 a	17. d	
18. b	18.d	18 e		18 e	18. a	
19. b	19.e	19 a		19 d	19. c	
20. b	20.d	20 b		20 b	20. e	
21. d		21 c		21 e	21. c	
		22 d		22 a	22. a	
		23 c		23 e	23. b	
				24 d	24. e	
				25 b	25. c	
				26 c	26. b	
				27 c		

Answer Key
Non Verbal Reasoning Question Types

Codes Key:

1 e
2 c
3 b
4 d
5 d
6 b
7 c
8 a
9 e
10 c
11 e
12 d
13 b
14 c
15 e

Hidden Shapes:

1 d
2 a
3 b
4 c
5 c
6 e
7 b
8 c
9 e
10 a
11 d
12 c
13 e
14 d
15 b
16 c
17 a
18 e
19 d
20 c
21 b

Combining Shapes:

1 c
2 a
3 d
4 b
5 e
6 c

Folding and Hole Punching:

1 c
2 b
3 e
4 d
5 a
6 d
7 b
8 c
9 e
10 d
11 d
12 c
13 e

Nets & Cubes:

1 a
2 d
3 e
4 e
5 a
6 a
7 c
8 b
9 e
10 c
11 a
12 d
13 b
14 c
15 c
16 e

2D View:

1 d
2 b
3 e
4 d
5 c

3D Blocks:

1 b
2 d
3 c
4 e
5 c

3D Rotation :

1 d
2 e
3 b
4 a
5 f
6 c

Answer Explanations

NVR : Odd one out

Question No 1.

Rule No 1. Each option has a circle

Rule No 2. Each option has a pentagon

Rule No 3. Each option has a rectangle

All options in this question obey the above-mentioned rules except Option C as it does not have a Rectangle, instead, it has a Hexagon.

Hence Option C is ODD in this question.

Question No 2.

Rule No 1. Each option has 5 sticks

Rule No 2. Each option has 2 sticks (out of 5 sticks) without a square head

Rule No 3. Each option has 3 sticks (out of 5 sticks) with a square head

All options in this question obey the above-mentioned rules except Option B as it has four sticks with a square head.

Hence Option B is ODD in this question.

Question No 3.

Rule No 1. Each option is divided into a diagonal.

Rule No 2. The direction of the diagonal does not matter in this question

Rule No 3. Each option has 2 total shapes i.e. one shape above and one below the diagonal.

All options in this question obey the above-mentioned rules except Option C as it has 3 shapes instead of 2 (2 shapes above and one below the diagonal)

Hence Option C is ODD in this question.

Question No 4.

Rule No 1. Each option has a hexagon shape.

Rule No 2. In each option, there are some lines on the upper and lower side of the hexagon, count them.

Rule No 3. Each option has small circles with a cross inside.

Rule No 4. In each option, the number of small circles (having a cross inside) is one less than the number of total lines outside the hexagon

All options in this question obey the above-mentioned rules except Option C as it has 4 lines outside the hexagon and 4 small circles inside whereas as per rule No 4, the small circles should be 3 instead of 4 in this option.

Hence Option C is ODD in this question.

Question No 5

Rule No 1. Each option has a diamond

Rule No 2. Each option has four different shapes at the corners of the diamond

Rule No 3. In each option, two shapes are in front and two are behind the diamond shapes.

All options in this question obey the above-mentioned rules except Option D as it has all four shapes in front of the diamond shape at its corners

Hence Option D is ODD in this question.

Question No 6

Rule No 1. Each cube has 9 small diamonds in it

Rule No 2. Each option has an odd number of filled diamonds

Rule No 3. Each option has an even number of empty diamonds

All options in this question obey the above-mentioned rules except Option A as it has an even number of filled and an odd number of empty diamonds. Hence Option A is ODD in this question.

Question No 7

Rule No 1. Each option has a square

Rule No 2. Each square has some diagonal lines at the corners and some circles inside

Rule No 3. Count the number of diagonal lines and circles, the diagonal lines are double as compared to the circle inside each square.

All options in this question obey the above-mentioned rules except Option D as it has 4 lines and 3 circles inside

Hence Option D is ODD in this question.

Question No 8

Rule No 1. Each option has a different type of shape.

Rule No 2. In each option, the shape is equally divided into four pieces

All options in this question obey the above-mentioned rules except Option D as after division its four segments are not equal in size.

Hence Option D is ODD in this question.

Question No 9

Rule No 1. Each option has a parallelogram

Rule No 2. Each parallelogram has one circle, 2 sticks with round heads and 2 plus signs inside it

Rule No 3. The direction of shapes inside each parallelogram does not matter in this question

All options in this question obey the above-mentioned rules except Option B as it has one plus sign instead of two

Hence Option B is ODD in this question.

Question No 10

Rule No 1. Each option has a fish mouth type shape and a circle inside the shape

Rule No 2. The position of the circle inside the shape is either at the upper side or at the lower side

All options in this question obey the above-mentioned rules except Option C as the position of the circle is in the middle of the shape

Hence Option C is ODD in this question.

Question No 11

Rule No 1. Each option has a pair of big stars and small stars inside them

Rule No 2. In each option, the number of small stars is equal in both the adjacent big stars

Rule No 3. In each option, the direction of the small stars is the same in both adjacent big stars

All options in this question obey the above-mentioned rules except Option D as it does not have the small stars in the same directions

Hence Option D is ODD in this question.

Question No 12

Rule No 1. Each option has a big square

Rule No 2. In each big square, starting from the upper left corner, there are 2 small squares, then a circle and a single square ending at the right lower corner

Rule No 3. The filling of shape does not matter in this question

All options in this question obey the above-mentioned rules except Option D as it does not have shapes in sequence i.e., a circle is after one square which should be after 2 squares

Hence Option D is ODD in this question.

Question No 13

Rule No 1. Each has a diamond in front and a filled square at the back

Rule No 2. Each option has an odd number of stars in it

All options in this question obey the above-mentioned rules except Option B as it has an even number of stars in it

Hence Option B is ODD in this question.

Question No 14

Rule No 1. Each option has a pentagon

Rule No 2. Each pentagon has a circle (with a cross inside) and an arrow

Rule No 3. In each option, the direction of the arrow is always outward from the circle (pointing against the circle)

All options in this question obey the above-mentioned rules except Option A as the arrow inside it is pointing towards the circle

Hence Option A is ODD in this question.

Question No 15

Rule No 1. Each option has a rectangle with round same-side corners

Rule No 2. Each option has two combined filled triangles and two sticks with round head

Rule No 3. In each rectangle, the combined triangles are always on the right side and two sticks are on the left side

Rule No 4. The direction of sticks does not matter in this question

All options in this question obey the above-mentioned rules except Option A as it has triangles on the left side and sticks on the right side

Hence Option A is ODD in this question.

Question No 16

Rule No 1. Each option has some arrows and stars

Rule No 2. The number of arrows and the number of stars are equal in each option

All options in this question obey the above-mentioned rules except Option B as it has three arrows and two stars

Hence Option B is ODD in this question.

Question No 17

Rule No 1. Each option has one triangle, one circle, one rectangle and one L-shape

Rule No 2. The direction of the triangle in each option is always pointing towards the right

Rule No 3. The position of shapes in each option does not matter in this question

All options in this question obey the above-mentioned rules except Option C as the triangle is pointing upward in this option

Hence Option C is ODD in this question.

Question No 18

In this question, each option has three objects except Option B which has four objects

Hence Option B is ODD in this question.

Question No 19

Rule No 1. Each option has two identical shapes, one is filled and one is empty

Rule No 2. The filled shape is always on the left side and the empty shape is on the right side in each option

All options in this question obey the above-mentioned rules except Option B as it has a filled shape on its right side and an empty on the left side

Hence Option B is ODD in this question.

Question No 20

Rule No 1. Each option has a plaque with a crescent and star inside

Rule No 2. In each option, there are circles outside at three corners of the plaque and one corner is empty

Rule No 3. The crescent and star are at the corner which is empty outside

All options in this question obey the above-mentioned rules except Option B as the crescent and star are not in the empty corner

Hence Option B is ODD in this question.

Question No 21

Rule No 1. Each option consists of a pentagon, a triangle, a square and a face.

Rule No 2. The direction of the face is upright to the adjacent corner

All options in this question obey the above-mentioned rules except Option D as the direction of his face is inverted

Hence Option D is ODD in this question.

NVR : Similarities

Question No 1.

Rule. Each shape on the question side has six corners

Option A – Incorrect: - This shape has five corners

Option B – Incorrect: - This shape has two corners

Option C – Correct: - This shape has six corners

Option D – Incorrect: - This shape has four corners

Option E – Incorrect: - This shape has twelve corners

Hence Option C is Correct.

Question No 2.

Rule. Each shape on the question side is of the same size as compared to its height and width

Option A – Incorrect: - This shape has a bigger width as compared to its height

Option B – Incorrect: - This shape has a bigger height as compared to its width

Option C – Correct: - This shape has the same size of width and height

Option D – Incorrect: - This shape has a bigger width as compared to its height

Option E – Incorrect: - This shape has a bigger height as compared to its width

Hence Option C is Correct.

Question No 3.

Rule. Each shape on the question side is a hexagon having a dotted hexagon inside

Option A – Incorrect: - This shape has a dotted hexagon outside

Option B – Incorrect: - This shape is a heptagon

Option C – Incorrect: - This shape is a triangle

Option D – Incorrect: - This shape is a trapezoid

Option E – Correct: - This shape is a hexagon with a dotted hexagon inside.

Hence Option E is Correct.

Question No 4.

Rule. Each shape on the question side has two unsymmetrical circles outside the shape and does not have any circle inside the shape.

Option A – Incorrect: - This shape has two circles outside and one inside

Option B – Incorrect: - This shape has no circles outside

Option C – Incorrect: - This shape has one circle outside

Option D – Incorrect: - This shape has three circles outside

Option E – Correct: - This shape has two circles outside.

Hence Option E is Correct.

Question No 5.

Rule. Each shape on the question side has one right angle

Option A – Incorrect: - This shape does not have a right angle

Option B – Incorrect: - This shape does not have a right angle

Option C – Correct: - This shape has a right angle

Option D – Incorrect: - This shape does not have a right angle

Option E – Incorrect: - This shape does not have a right angle

Hence Option C is Correct.

Question No 6.

Rule. Each shape on the question side is divided into two equal parts

Option A – Incorrect: - This shape has a bigger lower left part

Option B – Incorrect: - This shape has a bigger lower left part

Option C – Incorrect: - This shape has a smaller left-upper part

Option D – Incorrect: - This shape is divided into four parts

Option E – Correct: - This shape is divided into two equal parts.

Hence Option E is Correct.

Question No 7.

Rule. Each shape on the question side has some number of lines in the middle of the shape which are always equal to the corners of the shapes attached to that shape.

Option A – Incorrect: - This shape has one single line in the middle whereas the shape attached to it has four corners

Option B – Correct: - This shape has five lines in the middle and the shape attached to it has five corners

Option C – Incorrect: - This shape has two lines in the middle whereas the shape attached to it has no corners

Option D – Incorrect: - This shape has four lines in the middle whereas the shape attached to it has six corners

Option E – Incorrect: - This shape has no line in the middle whereas the shape attached to it has two corners

Hence Option B is Correct.

Question No 8.

Rule. Each shape on the question side has one duplicate shape but with a different filling style

Option A – Correct: - This shape has one duplicate shape (two stars) but with a different filling style

Option B – Incorrect: - All the three shapes are different in this option

Option C – Incorrect: - All three shapes are different in this option

Option D – Incorrect: - All three shapes are different in this option

Option E – Incorrect: - All three shapes are different in this option

Hence Option A is Correct.

Question No 9.

Rule. Each shape on the question side consists of two shapes. The corners of the outer shape are one more than the corners of the inner shape.

Option A – Incorrect: - The outer shape has seven corners whereas the inner shape has four corners

Option B – Incorrect: - The outer shape has five corners whereas the inner shape has three corners

Option C – Incorrect: - The outer shape has four corners whereas the inner shape has no corners

Option D – Incorrect: - The outer shape has four corners whereas the inner shape has two corners

Option E – Correct: - The outer shape has eight corners and the inner shape has seven corners

Hence Option E is Correct.

Question No 10.

Rule. Each shape on the question side has two diamonds on the right side of the stem and two on the left side of the stem. Moreover, the pot is cylindrical.

Option A – Incorrect: - This shape has three diamonds on either side of the stem

Option B – Incorrect: - This shape does not have a cylindrical pot

Option C – Incorrect: - This shape has two diamonds on one side and three diamonds on the other side of the stem

Option D – Correct: - This shape has two diamonds on the right side of the stem and two on the left side of the stem. Moreover, the pot is cylindrical.

Option E – Incorrect: - This shape has three diamonds on either side of the stem

Hence Option D is Correct.

Question No 11.

Rule. Each shape on the question side is divided into four equal parts

Option A – Incorrect: - This shape does not have four equal parts

Option B – Correct: - This shape is divided into four equal parts

Option C – Incorrect: - This shape does not have four equal parts

Option D – Incorrect: - This shape does not have four equal parts. The size of the left and right portions is bigger than the size of the upper and lower portions.

Option E – Incorrect: - This shape does not have four equal parts

Hence Option B is Correct.

Question No 12.

Rule. There is a tail in each shape on the question side

Option A – Incorrect: - This shape does not have a tail

Option B – Correct: - This shape has a tail

Option C – Incorrect: - This shape does not have a tail

Option D – Incorrect: - This shape does not have a tail

Option E – Incorrect: - This shape does not have a tail

Hence Option B is Correct.

Question No 13.

Rule. Each shape on the question side is divided into a diagonal. The corners of the shape on one side of the diagonal are equal to the corners of the shapes on the other side of the diagonal.

Option A – Incorrect: - The total number of corners of the shapes on either side of the diagonal is not equal.

Option B – Incorrect: - The total number of corners of the shapes on either side of the diagonal is not equal.

Option C – Incorrect: - The total number of corners of the shapes on either side of the diagonal is not equal.

Option D – Incorrect: - The total number of corners of the shapes on either side of the diagonal is not equal.

Option E – Correct: - The corners of the shape on one side of the diagonal are equal to the corners of the shapes on the other side of the diagonal.

Hence Option E is Correct.

Question No 14.

Rule. Each shape on the question side has some shapes inside. The total number of corners of inside shapes is twelve.

Option A – Incorrect: - The total number of corners of inside shapes is eleven.

Option B – Incorrect: - The total number of corners of inside shapes is twenty-four.

Option C – Incorrect: - The total number of corners of inside shapes is eighteen.

Option D – Correct: - The total number of corners of inside shapes is twelve.

Option E – Incorrect: - The total number of corners of inside shapes is sixteen.

Hence Option D is Correct.

Question No 15.

Rule. Each shape on the question side has a triangle in it.

Option A – Incorrect: - This shape does not have a triangle in it

Option B – Incorrect: - This shape does not have a triangle in it

Option C – Correct: - This shape has a triangle in it

Option D – Incorrect: - This shape does not have a triangle in it

Option E – Incorrect: - This shape does not have a triangle in it

Hence Option C is Correct.

Question No 16.

Rule. Each shape on the question side has two parallel pencils facing opposite to each other and one pencil has a greater width as compared to the other

Option A – Incorrect: - Two pencils in this shape are facing in the same direction

Option B – Correct: - Two pencils are facing opposite to each other and one pencil has greater width as compared to the other

Option C – Incorrect: - Two pencils are not parallel

Option D – Incorrect: - There are not two pencils in this shape.

Option E – Incorrect: - Parallel pencils are facing opposite however width of both pencils is the same.

Hence Option B is Correct.

Question No 17.

Rule. Each shape has one filled and three unfilled water drop

Option A – Incorrect: - This shape has two filled and two unfilled water drop

Option B – Correct: - This shape has one filled and three unfilled water drop

Option C – Incorrect: - This shape has two filled and two unfilled water drop

Option D – Incorrect: - This shape has two filled and two unfilled water drop

Option E – Incorrect: - This shape has two filled and one unfilled water drop

Hence Option B is Correct.

Question No 18.

Rule. Each shape on the question side is just behind the other in a sequential manner keeping only one shape in front and the rest are behind each other

Option A – Incorrect: - Two shapes are behind and two are in front

Option B – Incorrect: - One shape is behind and three are in front

Option C – Incorrect: - Two shapes are behind and two are in front

Option D – Correct: - Each shape is just behind the other in a sequential manner keeping only one shape in front and others are behind each other

Option E – Incorrect: - Two shapes are behind and two are in front

Hence Option D is Correct.

Question No 19.

Rule. Each shape on the question side has three shapes inside. The inside shapes are identical

Option A – Incorrect: - The inner shapes are not identical

Option B – Incorrect: - The inner shapes are not identical

Option C – Incorrect: - The inner shapes are not identical

Option D – Incorrect: - The inner shapes are not identical

Option E – Correct: - The inner shapes are identical

Hence Option E is Correct.

Question No 20.

Rule. Both the hearts on the question side are lying in the same size box

Option A – Incorrect: - The size of the heart box is not the same

Option B – Incorrect: - The size of the heart box is not the same

Option C – Incorrect: - The size of the heart box is not the same

Option D – Correct: - The size of the heart box is the same

Option E – Incorrect: - The size of the heart box is not the same

Hence Option D is Correct.

NVR : Reflection

Question No 1.

Rule. This shape has a horizontal reflection

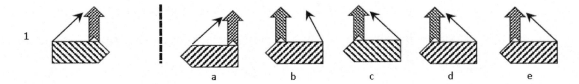

Option A – Incorrect: - Pentagon is correctly reflected however both the arrows are without reflection

Option B – Incorrect: - The Pentagon and broad arrow are reflected correctly however arrow has irrelevant space near its head.

Option C – Incorrect: - All shapes are reflected however inner lines of the pentagon are not affected by reflection.

Option D – Correct: - This shape is reflected correctly

Option E – Incorrect: - All shapes are reflected however inner lines of the broad arrow are not affected by reflection

Hence Option D is Correct.

Question No 2.

Rule. This shape has a horizontal reflection

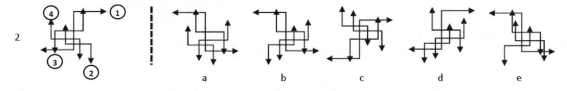

Option A – Incorrect: - Arrow No. 4 is not reflected correctly

Option B – Correct: - All the arrows are reflected correctly

Option C – Incorrect: - Arrow No. 1 is not reflected correctly

Option D – Incorrect: - Arrow No. 1 is not reflected correctly

Option E – Incorrect: - Arrow No. 4 is not reflected correctly

Hence Option B is Correct.

Question No 3.

Rule. This shape has a horizontal reflection

‸‒‒‒‒‒‒‒   a   b   c   d   E

Option A – Incorrect: - Face is not reflected

Option B – Incorrect: - Arrows are not reflected

Option C – Incorrect: - Everything is incorrectly reflected

Option D – Incorrect: - Diamond is reflected incorrectly

Option E – Correct: - Everything is correctly reflected

Hence Option E is Correct.

Question No 4.

Rule. This shape has a vertical reflection

a   b   c   d   e

Option A – Correct: The arrow and the heart are reflected vertically

Option B – Incorrect: - Shapes are not reflected, they are the same just like in the question

Option C – Incorrect: - Shapes are reflected vertically however lines in the heart are not reflected

Option D – Incorrect: - Lines in the arrow are incorrect

Option E – Incorrect: The arrow is vertically reflected whereas the heart is horizontally reflected

Hence Option A is Correct.

Question No 5.

Rule. This shape has a horizontal reflection

a   b   c   d   e

Option A – Incorrect: - Cube is not reflected

Option B – Incorrect: - Arrow is not reflected

Option C – Correct: - All shapes are reflected correctly

Option D – Incorrect: The arrow is not filled and lines are also in the wrong direction

Option E – Incorrect: - Lines inside the hexagon are in the wrong direction

Hence Option C is Correct.

Question No 6.

Rule. This shape has a vertical reflection

 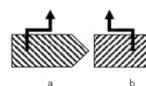

a   b   c   d   e

Option A – Incorrect: - Lines inside the Pentagon are not reflected

Option B – Incorrect: - Arrow shape is not reflected vertically

Option C – Incorrect: - Pentagon is reflected horizontally

Option D – Correct: - This shape is reflected correctly

Option E – Incorrect: - Pentagon is reflected horizontally

Hence Option D is Correct.

Question No 7.

Rule. This shape has a horizontal reflection

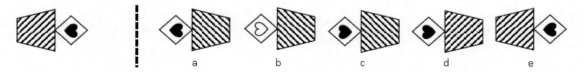

Option A – Incorrect: - Heart is not reflected horizontally

Option B – Incorrect: - Heart is empty

Option C – Correct: - All shapes are reflected correctly

Option D – Incorrect: - Lines inside the trapezoid are not reflected horizontally

Option E – Incorrect: - This shape is not reflected at all, it is the same just like question

Hence Option C is Correct.

Question No 8.

Rule. This shape has a horizontal reflection

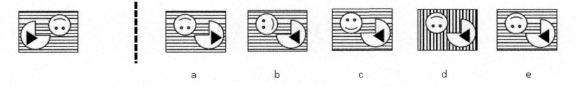

Option A – Incorrect: - Triangle is not reflected correctly

Option B – Incorrect: - Face is not reflected correctly

Option C – Incorrect: - Face is not reflected at all

Option D – Incorrect: - Lines inside the square are in the wrong direction

Option E – Correct: - Everything is correctly reflected

Hence Option E is Correct.

Question No 9.

Rule. This shape has a vertical reflection

a b c d e

Option A – Incorrect: - The shape is not reflected vertically

Option B – Correct: - The shape is reflected correctly

Option C – Incorrect: - The shape is not reflected vertically

Option D – Incorrect: - The chevron is not reflected vertically

Option E – Incorrect: - The lightning is not reflected at all

Hence Option B is Correct.

Question No 10.

Rule. This shape has a horizontal reflection

a b c d e

Option A – Correct: - Correct horizontal reflection of the shape

Option B – Incorrect: - Crescent is not reflected

Option C – Incorrect: - Triangle is not reflected

Option D – Incorrect: - Crescent is not reflected

Option E – Incorrect: - Arrow and Crescent are not reflected

Hence Option A is Correct.

Question No 11.

Rule. This shape has a vertical reflection

a   b   c   d   e

Option A – Incorrect: - Shape is not reflected vertically

Option B – Incorrect: - All shapes except triangle are not reflected correctly

Option C – Correct: - All shapes are reflected correctly

Option D – Incorrect: - Triangle is not reflected vertically

Option E – Incorrect: - Triangle is not reflected vertically and other shapes also have reflection error

Hence Option C is Correct.

Question No 12.

Rule. This shape has a horizontal reflection

a   b   c   d   e

Option A – Incorrect: - Stick No. 1 is not reflected correctly

Option B – Incorrect: - Triangle is not reflected correctly

Option C – Incorrect: - Arrow is not reflected correctly

Option D – Correct: - This shape is reflected correctly

Option E – Incorrect: - Stick No. 2 is not reflected correctly

Hence Option D is Correct.

Question No 13.

Rule. This shape has a vertical reflection

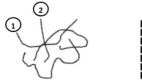 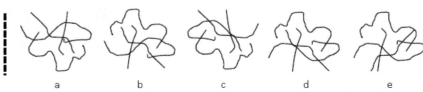

Option A – Incorrect: - The shape is not vertically reflected

Option B – Incorrect: - The shape marked as 1 is changed in this option

Option C – Incorrect: - The shape is not vertically reflected

Option D – Correct: - This shape is reflected correctly

Option E – Incorrect: - The shape marked as 1 is changed in this option

Hence Option D is Correct.

Question No 14.

Rule. This shape has a horizontal reflection

Option A – Incorrect: - The triangle is not reflected

Option B – Incorrect: - The diagonal lines are not reflected

Option C – Correct: - All shapes are reflected correctly

Option D – Incorrect: - The dotted pattern is changed

Option E – Incorrect: - Lines in the circle are not reflected

Hence Option C is Correct.

Question No 15.

Rule. This shape has a vertical reflection

---------- a b c d e

Option A – Incorrect: - The shape is not vertically reflected

Option B – Incorrect: - The shape is not vertically reflected

Option C – Correct: - All shapes are reflected vertically in a correct manner

Option D – Incorrect: - The cylindrical shape is not reflected vertically

Option E – Incorrect: - The crescent is not reflected correctly

Hence Option C is Correct.

Question No 16.

Rule. This shape has a horizontal reflection

a b c d e

Option A – Incorrect: - Circle with diagonal is not reflected

Option B – Incorrect: - The shape is not reflected horizontally

Option C – Incorrect: - Face is incorrectly reflected

Option D – Incorrect: - Cloud is reflected incorrectly

Option E – Correct: - Everything is correctly reflected

Hence Option E is Correct.

Question No 17.

Rule. This shape has a vertical reflection

-------   a   b   c   d   e

Option A – Incorrect: - Lines inside the Pentagon are not reflected correctly

Option B – Correct: - Everything is reflected correctly

Option C – Incorrect: - Lines inside the pentagon and trapezoid are not reflected correctly

Option D – Incorrect: The dotted pattern in the arrow is not correct

Option E – Incorrect: - The shape is not vertically reflected

Hence Option B is Correct.

Question No 18.

Rule. This shape has a horizontal reflection

           a   b   c   d   e

Option A – Incorrect: - Sun is not filled

Option B – Incorrect: - Lines direction around the face is incorrect

Option C – Incorrect: - Face is incorrectly reflected

Option D – Incorrect: The direction of dotted lines around the sun is incorrect

Option E – Correct: - Everything is correctly reflected

Hence Option E is Correct.

Question No 19.

Rule. This shape has a horizontal reflection

  |

a   b   c   d   e

Option A – Correct: - The shape is reflected correctly

Option B – Incorrect: - The direction of lines in the arrow is incorrect

Option C – Incorrect: - The circles have a cross sign instead of a plus sign

Option D – Incorrect: The diamond is filled with the wrong pattern

Option E – Incorrect: - Arrow is not reflected horizontally

Hence **Option A** is Correct.

Question No 20.

Rule. This shape has a horizontal reflection

 |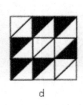

a   b   c   d   e

Option A – Incorrect: The left box in the middle row is wrong

Option B – Correct: - The shape is reflected correctly

Option C – Incorrect: The middle box in the middle row is wrong

Option D – Incorrect: The middle box in the middle row is wrong

Option E – Incorrect: The middle box in the upper row is wrong

Hence **Option B** is Correct.

Question No 21.

Rule. This shape has a horizontal reflection

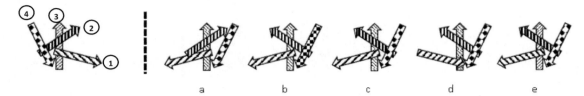

Option A – Incorrect: - Arrow No. 2 is not reflected

Option B – Incorrect: - The dotted pattern in arrow No. 4 is wrong

Option C – Correct: - All shapes are reflected correctly

Option D – Incorrect: - Arrow No. 1 is not reflected

Option E – Incorrect: - The direction of lines in arrow No. 3 is wrong

Hence Option C is Correct.

Question No 22.

Rule. This shape has a vertical reflection

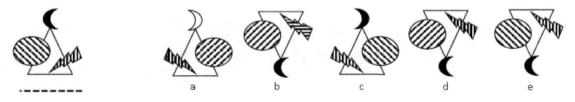

Option A – Incorrect: - The shape is not reflected vertically

Option B – Incorrect: - The direction of lines in lightning is wrong

Option C – Incorrect: - The shape is not reflected vertically

Option D – Correct: - This shape is reflected correctly

Option E – Incorrect: - The direction of lines in the circle is wrong

Hence Option D is Correct.

Question No 23.

Rule. This shape has a horizontal reflection

a   b   c   d   e

Option A – Incorrect: - Lower most shape is not reflected

Option B – Incorrect: The shape inside the hexagon is not reflected

Option C – Correct: - All shapes are reflected correctly

Option D – Incorrect: - The uppermost shape is reflected incorrectly

Option E – Incorrect: - The Z-shaped line is not reflected

Hence Option C is Correct.

NVR : Analogy

Question No 1.

Rule No 1. The shape turns 90° clockwise

Rule No 2. All small shapes inside the big shape come out from the adjacent line

Rule No 3. The shapes which come out from the main shape become unfilled and inverted.

Rule No 4. The main shape becomes filled

Option A – Incorrect: - Does not obey rule No 4.

Option B – Incorrect: - Does not obey rules 4 & 3.

Option C – Incorrect: - Does not obey rule No 3.

Option D – Correct: - This shape obeys all the above rules.

Option E – Incorrect: - Does not obey rule No 3.

Hence Option D is Correct.

Question No 2.

Rule No 1. The shape turns 45° clockwise

Rule No 2. Nothing changes in the inner shapes

Rule No 3. Nothing changes with the outer shapes.

Option A – Incorrect: - Does not obey rule No 2.

Option B – Incorrect: - Does not obey rule No 1.

Option C – Correct: - This shape obeys all the above rules.

Option D – Incorrect: - Does not obey rule No. 1.

Option E – Incorrect: - Does not obey rule No 3.

Hence **Option C** is Correct.

Question No 3.

Rule No 1. Three small shapes on one side of the main shape, shift to the opposite side

Rule No 2. One small shape on one side of the main shape shifts to the opposite side and rotates 90° anticlockwise

Rule No 3. The position and rotation of the shape in the centre do not change.

Rule No 4. The arrow rotates 180° clockwise

Option A – Correct: - This shape obeys all the above rules.

Option B – Incorrect: - Does not obey rule No 2.

Option C – Incorrect: - Does not obey rule No 4.

Option D – Incorrect: - Does not obey rule No 4.

Option E – Incorrect: - Does not obey rule No 2.

Hence **Option A** is Correct.

Question No 4.

Rule No 1. The left shape turns 90° clockwise and its filling pattern does not change

Rule No 2. The right side shape inverts vertically and its filling pattern changes just like (a) horizontal lines change to vertical (b) upward diagonal changes to downward diagonals

Option A – Incorrect: - Does not obey rules No 1 & 2.

Option B – Incorrect: - Does not obey rules No 1 & 2.

Option C – Correct: - This shape obeys all the above rules.

Option D – Incorrect: - Does not obey rules No 1 & 2.

Option E – Incorrect: - Does not obey rules No 1 & 2.

Hence Option C is Correct.

Question No 5.

Rule No 1. The complete shape inverts vertically

Rule No 2. The shape in the middle becomes filled

Rule No 3. After inversion, the upper shape adopts the same filling pattern as the lower shape and vice versa

Rule No 4. The shape on the left becomes unfilled

Option A – Incorrect: - Does not obey rule No 1.

Option B – Incorrect: - Does not obey rule No 3.

Option C – Incorrect: - Does not obey rule No 3.

Option D – Incorrect: - The center shape is changed which should not be as per the rules.

Option E – Correct: - This shape obeys all the above rules.

Hence Option E is Correct.

Question No 6.

Rule No 1. The shape is vertically inverted

Rule No 2. Nothing changes in the shape except rule No. 1.

Option A – Incorrect: The filling pattern of the oval shape is not the same.

Option B – Correct: - This shape obeys all the above rules.

Option C – Incorrect: - Does not obey rule No 1 and 2.

Option D – Incorrect: - Heart is not inverted as per rule No. 1.

Option E – Incorrect: - Arrow is not inverted as per rule No. 1

Hence **Option B** is Correct.

Question No 7.

Rule No 1. The shape at the inner side comes out at the outermost position

Rule No 2. The shape on the outer side goes inside without inversion

Rule No 3. The shape at the top becomes unfilled when it goes inside.

Option A – Correct: - This shape obeys all the above rules.

Option B – Incorrect: - Does not obey rule No 3.

Option C – Incorrect: - The outermost shape is changed which should not be so as per rule No. 1.

Option D – Incorrect: - The shapes are changed from the question shape.

Option E – Incorrect: - The inner shape is inverted and does not obey rule No. 2.

Hence **Option A** is Correct.

Question No 8.

Rule No 1. The incomplete shape becomes complete

Rule No 2. The position/rotation/shape/filling pattern of the inner shape remains the same

Rule No 3. The outer shape comes inside the adjacent point inverts vertically and fills with a light gray shade

Option A – Incorrect: - Does not obey rule No 2.

Option B – Incorrect: - Does not obey rule No 3.

Option C – Incorrect: - Does not obey rule No 2.

Option D – Incorrect: - Does not obey rule No 3.

Option E – Correct: - This shape obeys all the above rules.

Hence Option E is Correct.

Question No 9.

Rule No 1. The shape on the left divides into two halves vertically

Rule No 2. The shape on the right separates itself from the left shape and its upper portion becomes unfilled whereas the filling pattern of the lower side remains the same

Rule No 3. The arrow flips vertically

Option A – Incorrect: - Does not obey rule No 2.

Option B – Incorrect: - Does not obey rule No 2.

Option C – Correct: - This shape obeys all the above rules.

Option D – Incorrect: - Does not obey rule No 3.

Option E – Incorrect: - Does not obey rule No 1.

Hence Option C is Correct.

Question No 10.

Rule No 1. The shape inverts vertically

Rule No 2. After inversion, the inverted shape joins vertically to the original shape keeping the upper and the lower distance the same

Rule No 3. The inverted shape positions itself at the lower side

Option A – Incorrect: - Does not obey rule No 1.

Option B – Incorrect: - Does not obey rule No 3.

Option C – Incorrect: - The outer upper shape is different.

Option D – Correct: - This shape obeys all the above rules.

Option E – Incorrect: - The outer lower shape is different.

Hence **Option D** is Correct.

Question No 11.

Rule No 1. The outer shape becomes filled with a solid black colour

Rule No 2. The inner shape turns to a shape having 2 corners more than the question inner shape

Rule No 3. The inner shape does not rotate

Option A – Incorrect: - Does not obey rule No 1.

Option B – Incorrect: - Does not obey rule No 2.

Option C – Correct: - This shape obeys all the above rules.

Option D – Incorrect: - Does not obey rule No. 1.

Option E – Incorrect: - Does not obey rule No 3.

Hence **Option C** is Correct.

Question No 12.

Rule No 1. The divided two halves join and become a square

Rule No 2. The shape on the left half becomes the middle shape in the resultant shape and its border turns dotted.

Rule No 3. The shape on the right half becomes the innermost shape and it is filled with a solid black colour.

Option A – Incorrect: - Does not obey rule No 3.

Option B – Incorrect: - Middle shape is filled which is not required.

Option C – Incorrect: - Does not obey rule No 3.

Option D – Incorrect: The outer shape has a dotted line which is not required

Option E – Correct: - This shape obeys all the above rules.

Hence **Option E** is Correct.

Question No 13.

Rule No 1. Black-filled boxes are turned to grey-filled and vice versa

Rule No 2. Horizontal lines filled boxes are changed into vertically filled lines and vice versa

Rule No 3. Boxes with upward diagonals are changed with downward diagonals and vice versa.

Rule No 4. White boxes remain unchanged

Option A – Incorrect: - Especially, the upper row, box no 2 from right does not obey Rule No. 1.

Option B – Incorrect: - Especially, upper row, box no 4 from right does not obey Rule No 1.

Option C – Incorrect: - Especially, the upper row, box no 1 from the right does not obey Rule No 1.

Option D – Incorrect: - Especially, lowest row, box no 3 from the right does not obey Rule No 2

Option E – Correct: - This shape obeys all the above rules.

Hence **Option E** is Correct.

Question No 14.

Rule No 1. The shape horizontally flips

Rule No 2. The flipped shape joins with the original shape horizontally keeping the centre of both shapes on the same point

Rule No 3. Both shapes do not change their colour or shape.

Option A – Incorrect: - Does not obey rule No 3.

Option B – Incorrect: - Does not obey rule No 2.

Option C – Incorrect: - Does not obey rule No 2.

Option D – Correct: - This shape obeys all the above rules.

Option E – Incorrect: - Does not obey rule No 3.

Hence **Option D** is Correct.

Question No 15.

Rule No 1. The complete shape flips vertically

Rule No 2. Position/colour/rotation/size of shapes do not change in the resultant shape

Option A – Incorrect: - The circle is in the wrong place.

Option B – Correct: - This shape obeys all the above rules.

Option C – Incorrect: - The chevron is not inverted.

Option D – Incorrect: - The diagonal brackets are wrongly inverted.

Option E – Incorrect: - The face is not inverted.

Hence **Option B** is Correct.

Question No 16.

Rule No 1. The shape is filled with a dark grey shade

Rule No 2. Lines inside the small shapes are rotated 90° and do not change their pattern

Rule No 3. The small inside shapes do not change their position/rotation/size/shape/colour

Option A – Incorrect: - Lines inside the donut shape do not obey rule No 2

Option B – Incorrect: - Does not obey rule No 1.

Option C – Correct: - This shape obeys all the above rules.

Option D – Incorrect: - Lines inside the Pentagon do not obey rule No. 2.

Option E – Incorrect: - Lines inside the diamond do not obey rule No. 2.

Hence Option C is Correct.

Question No 17.

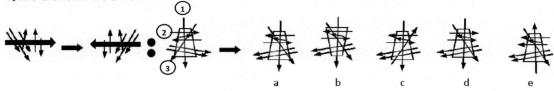

a   b   c   d   e

Rule No 1. The complete shape is inverted horizontally

Option A – Correct: - This shape is inverted horizontally.

Option B – Incorrect: - Arrow No. 2 is not perfectly placed.

Option C – Incorrect: - Arrow No. 3 is not perfectly placed.

Option D – Incorrect: - Arrow No. 2 is not inverted horizontally.

Option E – Incorrect: - Arrow No. 1 is in the wrong direction

Hence Option A is Correct.

Question No 18.

Rule No 1. An inner shape is introduced and the number of corners of the inner shape is equal to the number of diamonds in the question shape,

Rule No 2. The inner shape is filled with downward diagonals

Option A – Incorrect: - Does not obey rule No 2.

Option B – Incorrect: - Does not obey rule No 2.

Option C – Incorrect: - Does not obey rule No. 1.

Option D – Incorrect: - Does not obey rule No. 1.

Option E – Correct: - This shape obeys all the above rules.

Hence **Option E** is Correct.

Question No 19.

Rule No 1. The big shape rotates 90° clockwise but does not change its appearance/structure

Rule No 2. The shape in the centre of the big shape rotates 90° clockwise and comes out from the big shape

Rule No 3. The smaller shapes at the ups and downsides of the middle shape go inside the middle shape and interchange their positions.

Rule No 4. The smaller shapes only interchange their position in the resultant shape however they are not changed with respect to their size/ colour/rotation

Rule No 5. The right half portion of the main shape is filled with the same pattern as the middle shape and its filling design does not changes

Rule No 6. The middle shape becomes unfilled

Option A – Incorrect: - Does not obey rule No. 4, the triangle is inverted.

Option B – Incorrect: - Does not obey rule No 1.

Option C – Incorrect: - Does not obey rule No. 3.

Option D – Correct: - This shape obeys all the above rules.

Option E – Incorrect: - Does not obey rule No 5.

Hence **Option D** is Correct.

Question No 20.

Rule No 1. The shape in the corner of the main shape shifts to the next corner anticlockwise

Rule No 2. The corner shape is filled with upward diagonals

Rule No 3. The arrowhead is changed with the Diamond Head.

Option A – Incorrect: - Does not obey rule No 1.

Option B – Correct: - This shape obeys all the above rules.

Option C – Incorrect: - Does not obey rule No 2.

Option D – Incorrect: - Does not obey rule No. 1.

Option E – Incorrect: - Does not obey rule No 3.

Hence **Option B** is Correct.

Question No 21.

Rule No 1. The outermost shapes remain the same and do not change their position/rotation/colour/appearance

Rule No 2. The two shapes come out from the bigger shape at the top of it.

Rule No 3. The inner shapes, when come out, interchange their position i.e. the innermost becomes outer and the outer becomes innermost.

Rule No 4. The colour/appearance/rotation/pattern of inner shapes do not change

Option A – Incorrect: - Does not obey rule No 4.

Option B – Incorrect: - Does not obey rule No 1.

Option C – Incorrect: - Does not obey rule No 4.

Option D – Incorrect: - Does not obey rule No 3.

Option E – Correct: - This shape obeys all the above rules.

Hence **Option E** is Correct.

Question No 22.

Rule No 1. The shape rotates 90° anticlockwise

Rule No 2. The shape is doubled.

Rule No 3. After rule No 1&2, a small right portion of the shape is removed.

Option A – Correct: - This shape obeys all the above rules.

Option B – Incorrect: - Does not obey rule No 1.

Option C – Incorrect: - Does not obey rule No 3.

Option D – Incorrect: - Does not obey rule No 3.

Option E – Incorrect: - Does not obey rule No 1.

Hence Option A is Correct.

Question No 23.

Rule No 1. The bigger shape does not change its appearance/position/rotation/colour/size

Rule No 2. In the resultant shape, a new shape is introduced that has corners equal to the dots in the question shape.

Rule No 3. The newly introduced shape is filled with dark black colour.

Rule No 4. In the resultant shape, the number of dots and corners are equal

Option A – Incorrect: - Does not obey rules No 2&3.

Option B – Incorrect: - Does not obey rules No 4&3.

Option C – Incorrect: - Does not obey rule No 2.

Option D – Incorrect: - Does not obey rules No 3&4.

Option E – Correct: - This shape obeys all the above rules.

Hence Option E is Correct.

Question No 24.

Rule No 1. The border style of the inner shape changes with the border style of the outer shape and vice versa

Rule No 2. The inner shape rotates 90° clockwise

Option A – Incorrect: - Does not obey rule No 2.

Option B – Incorrect: - Does not obey rule No 1.

Option C – Incorrect: - Does not obey rule No. 1.

Option D – Correct: - This shape obeys all the above rules.

Option E – Incorrect: - Does not obey rule No 1.

Hence **Option D** is Correct.

Question No 25.

Rule No 1. The bigger shape does not change its appearance/position/rotation/colour/size

Rule No 2. The shape in the bottom of the bigger shape does not change its appearance/position/rotation/colour/size/filling pattern

Rule No 3. The shape on the top of the bigger shape (a) comes completely inside to the adjacent point (b) inverts vertically and (c) is filled with a grey colour

Option A – Incorrect: - Does not obey rule No 3c.

Option B – Correct: - This shape obeys all the above rules.

Option C – Incorrect: - Does not obey rule No 2.

Option D – Incorrect: - Does not obey rule No 3a.

Option E – Incorrect: - Does not obey rule No 3c.

Hence **Option B** is Correct.

Question No 26.

Rule No 1. The main shape divides into two halves

Rule No 2. The below half is removed

Rule No 3. The upper half is inverted in joined below the lower half keeping the lower half in front.

Option A – Incorrect: - Does not obey rule No 1.

Option B – Incorrect: - Does not obey rule No 3.

Option C – Correct: - This shape obeys all the above rules.

Option D – Incorrect: - Does not obey rule No 3.

Option E – Incorrect: - Does not obey rule No 3.

Hence **Option C** is Correct.

Question No 27.

Rule No 1. The black filled box turns into grey filled box and vice versa

Rule No 2. The horizontal lines in the box changes to vertical and vice versa

Rule No 3. The upward diagonal lines in any box change with downward diagonal lines and vice versa.

Rule No 4. Except for changes mentioned in Rules No 1, 2 & 3, all boxes remain unchanged.

Option A – Incorrect: - The upper rightmost box does not obey rule 1.

Option B – Incorrect: - In the upper row, the 2nd box from the right does not obey rule No. 1.

Option C – Correct: - This shape obeys all the above rules.

Option D – Incorrect: - The upper rightmost box does not obey rule 1.

Option E – Incorrect: - Many boxes do not obey the all above rules.

Hence **Option C** is Correct.

NVR : Series

1. B - the shape is only rotating 45 degrees each time

2. D - the pattern moves down one shape each time

3. In this question, the only symmetry is the arrow, either double-sided or single-sided. So the correct option is D

4. A - the circle is moving from the sides of the rectangle to the corner the shape will turn either grey or dark grey in this case

5. C - the shape has rotated but not as much as the third pattern and the circle has moved slightly down the middle of the rectangles

6. D - the arrows increase by one as we do through the sequence (the answer is not e because the dots on the arrows slowly drift to the right but the dots option e drift slowly to the left)

7. In this question, each option (on the question side) has 11 corners. So according to this rule option B is correct.

8. C - the small arrow turns 45 degrees each time the shapes around the small arrow are just there as a distraction

9. B - the only possible answer is b as each pattern in the sequence has a dotted triangle with a double headed arrow as its base

10. the filled pattern of each shape is considered. Moreover, the filled pattern should also have the right direction. So according to these rules option E is correct.

11. D - the long line of circles change their pattern from white black white black white to black white black white black and the arrows on either side mirror the position of the previous pattern

12. C - the dots on the side of the shape increase once and the top dots increase but remain as three

13. D - this is the only possible answer as it the only one that follows the rules of the sequence which is no shape should be the same and it is the only one that uses the original patterns

14. E - the two shapes have already made their complete turn which means they go back to their original positons which is the positons at the start of the sequence

15. A - you can see that the cross on the left of the shape goes up one each time and the shape to the left rotates 90 degrees anti-clcokwise each time

16. B - the heart will travel to each side of the shape while that dot would travel to the side and the curved sides of the shape and the two wavy lines travel diagonally from corner to corner

17. D the amount of white squares decrease by 1 each time

18. A the double headed arrow moves along the sides of the hexagon while the cross moves from corner to corner and the oval goes from one corner skips one and goes to the next

Question No 19.

Rule No 1. Each shape rotates 30° clockwise as compared to its previous shape

Rule No 2. In alternate shape, the single-sided arrow in the middle becomes double-sided

Rule No 3. The cross sign turns into filled with solid black colour in alternative shapes.

Option A – Incorrect: - Does not obey rule No 3.

Option B – Incorrect: - Does not obey rule No 1.

Option C – Correct: - This shape obeys all the above rules.

Option D – Incorrect: - Does not obey rule 2.

Option E – Incorrect: - Does not obey rules 1&3.

Hence **Option C** is Correct.

Question No 20.

Rule No 1. The shape rotates 90° clockwise

Rule No 2. Nothing changes in the shape except rule No. 1

Option A – Incorrect: - Does not obey rule No 2.

Option B – Incorrect: - Does not obey rule No 2.

Option C – Incorrect: - Does not obey rule No 2.

Option D – Incorrect: - Does not obey rule No 2.

Option E – Correct: - This shape obeys all the above rules.

Hence **Option E** is Correct.

Question No 21.

Rule No 1. The filled pattern in each next shape changes in a sequence

Rule No 2. The sequence of the filled pattern is shingle, then diagonal bricks, then vertical lines, then upward diagonal lines and after this, it repeats

Hence in blank shape, the filled pattern should be diagonal bricks

Therefore Option C is Correct.

Question No 22.

Rule No 1. The diagonals in the centre boxes change their directs (from upward to downward and vice versa) in each next shape

Rule No 2. The smaller shapes inside the upper portion of the bigger shape change its position with the shape present in the lower portion and vice versa in each next shape

Rule No 3. The smaller shapes inside only interchange their positions, their appearance/colour/size/filling design does not change

Option A – Correct: - This shape obeys all the above rules.

Option B – Incorrect: - Does not obey rule No 2.

Option C – Incorrect: - Does not obey rules No 1&2.

Option D – Incorrect: - Does not obey rule No 3.

Option E – Incorrect: - Does not obey rule No 3.

Hence Option A is Correct.

Question No 23.

Rule No 1. The shape flips vertically

Rule No 2. A single smaller shape on one side of the line is copied to the other side of the same line in a resultant shape.

Rule No 3. Nothing changes except changes mentioned in Rules No 1&2.

Option A – Incorrect: - Does not obey rule No 2 (single line).

Option B – Correct: - This shape obeys all the above rules.

Option C – Incorrect: - Does not obey rule No 3.

Option D – Incorrect: - Does not obey rule No 3.

Option E – Incorrect: - Does not obey rule No 3.

Hence Option B is Correct.

Question No 24.

In the upper box, one line is extra as compared to its adjacent lower box

The last lower box has 9 lines, hence the blank box should have 10 lines in it.

Therefore Option E is Correct.

Question No 25.

Rule No 1. The complete is vertically inverted

Rule No 2. Each shape has one extra double-sided arrow as compared to its previous shape

Option A – Incorrect: - Does not obey rule No 2.

Option B – Incorrect: - Does not obey rule No 1.

Option C – Correct: - This shape obeys all the above rules.

Option D – Incorrect: - Does not obey rule 2.

Option E – Incorrect: - Does not obey rule 2.

Hence Option C is Correct.

Question No 26.

Rule No 1. Each shape is inverted vertically

Rule No 2. There is a small square box in the upper boxes

Rule No 3. There is a small diamond box in the lower boxes.

Rule No 4. The small filled circle is the same throughout the boxes

Option A – Incorrect: - Does not obey rule No 2.

Option B – Correct: - This shape obeys all the above rules.

Option C – Incorrect: - Does not obey rule No 4.

Option D – Incorrect: - Does not obey rule No 3.

Option E – Incorrect: - Does not obey rule No 3.

Hence **Option B** is Correct.

NVR : Matrices

Question No 1.

Rule No 1. This matrix has a vertical reflection into the opposite box

Rule No 2. The lines change from solid to dashed and vice versa in the opposite box

Rule No 3. Position/size/rotation/appearance of small shapes do not change except its vertical inversion.

Option A – Correct: - This shape obeys all above stated rules

Option B – Incorrect: - Does not obey Rule No 2

Option C – Incorrect: - Does not obey Rule No 3

Option D – Incorrect: - Does not obey Rule No 3

Option E – Incorrect: - Does not obey Rule No 3

Hence Option A is Correct.

Question No 2.

Rule No 1. This matrix has horizontal changing shapes

Rule No 2. Each row has one of the four shapes, no duplicate shape

Rule No 3. The reflection/size/rotation/appearance of shapes in each row do not change except its position.

Option A – Incorrect: - Does not obey Rule No 2

Option B – Correct: - This shape obeys all above stated rules

Option C – Incorrect: - Does not obey Rule No 2

Option D – Incorrect: - Does not obey Rule No. 3, there are three downward diagonals instead of four

Option E – Incorrect: - Does not obey Rule No 2

Hence Option B is Correct.

Question No 3.

Rule No 1. This matrix has horizontal changing shapes

Rule No 2. Each row has one of the four shapes, no duplicate shape

Rule No 3. The reflection/size/rotation/appearance of shapes in each row do not change except its position.

Rule No 4. Circles are produced in each box so that it makes a square of four circles.

Option A – Incorrect: - Does not obey Rule No 3

Option B – Incorrect: - Does not obey Rule No 2

Option C – Incorrect: - Does not obey Rule No 2

Option D – Incorrect: - Does not obey Rule No 4

Option E – Correct: - This shape obeys all above stated rules

Hence Option E is Correct.

Question No 4.

Rule No 1. This matrix divides a complete shape into nine segments

Rule No 2. The four edge boxes of the matrix have 3 sets of arrows (at the outer side inside the box) rotating clockwise

Rule No 3. The 3 sets of arrows face opposite alternatively.

Rule No 4. These edge boxes have two diagonal lines perpendicular to the arrows

Option A – Incorrect: - Does not obey Rule No 3

Option B – Incorrect: - Does not obey Rule No 4

Option C – Correct: - This shape obeys all above stated rules

Option D – Incorrect: - Irrelevant shape in the box

Option E – Incorrect: - Does not obey Rule No 2

Hence Option C is Correct.

Question No 5.

Rule No 1. This matrix has horizontal and diagonal shapes in sequence

Rule No 2. The shape in the middle box doubles for both diagonals

Rule No 3. Inversion/size/rotation/appearance of shapes do not change except their position.

Rule No 4. Each row has one of the three shapes without duplication except rule No. 2.

Option A – Incorrect: - Does not obey Rule No 4

Option B – Correct: - This shape obeys all above stated rules

Option C – Incorrect: - Does not obey Rule No 4

Option D – Incorrect: - Does not obey Rule No 3

Option E – Incorrect: - Does not obey Rule No 4

Hence Option B is Correct.

Question No 6.

Rule No 1. This matrix has a horizontal changing shape sequence

Rule No 2. Each row has one of the three shapes, no duplicate shape

Rule No 3. The reflection/size/rotation/appearance of shapes in each row do not change except its position.

Option A – Incorrect: - Does not obey Rule No 2

Option B – Incorrect: - Does not obey Rule No 3

Option C – Incorrect: - Does not obey Rule No 2&3

Option D – Correct: - This shape obeys all above stated rules

Option E – Incorrect: - Does not obey Rule No 3

Hence Option D is Correct.

Question No 7.

Rule No 1. This matrix has a horizontal changing shape sequence

Rule No 2. Each row has one of the three shapes, no duplicate shape

Rule No 3. The reflection/size/rotation/appearance of shapes in each row do not change except its position.

Option A – Incorrect: - Does not obey Rule No 3

Option B – Correct: - This shape obeys all above stated rules

Option C – Incorrect: - Does not obey Rule No 2

Option D – Incorrect: - Does not obey Rule No 3

Option E – Incorrect: - Does not obey Rule No 2

Hence Option B is Correct.

Question No 8.

Rule No 1. This matrix has a horizontal adjacent box pattern

Rule No 2. The arrow in the corner rotates 180° and shifts to the opposite corner

Rule No 3. The upper two horizontal shapes change vertically.

Rule No 4. After changing vertically, the upper shape has the filled pattern of the lowermost shape in the question box

Rule No 5. After changing vertically, the lower shape has the filled pattern of the middle shape in the question box

Option A – Incorrect: - Does not obey Rule No 2

Option B – Incorrect: - Does not obey Rule No 2

Option C – Incorrect: - Does not obey Rule No 2&3

Option D – Correct: - This shape obeys all above stated rules

Option E – Incorrect: - Does not obey Rule No 2

Hence Option D is Correct.

Question No 9.

Rule No 1. This matrix has a horizontal adjacent box pattern

Rule No 2. The arrow goes one step behind and keeps the pattern of the shape same

Rule No 3. The box-type shape remains the same and it does not change with respect to rotation/appearance/direction

Option A – Incorrect: - Does not obey Rule No 2

Option B – Correct: - This shape obeys all above stated rules

Option C – Incorrect: - Does not obey Rule No 2

Option D – Incorrect: - Does not obey Rule No 2

Option E – Incorrect: - Does not obey Rule No 3

Hence Option B is Correct.

Question No 10.

Rule No 1. This matrix has a horizontal adjacent box pattern

Rule No 2. The uppermost shape moves to the lower side

Rule No 3. The shape beneath the diamonds changes its quantity equal to the number of diamonds.

Rule No 4. The diamonds disappear in the resultant shape

Rule No 5. Reflection/size/rotation/appearance/filling pattern of shapes do not change except their position

Option A – Incorrect: - Does not obey Rule No 4

Option B – Incorrect: - Does not obey Rule No 2

Option C – Incorrect: - Does not obey Rule No 2&4

Option D – Incorrect: - Does not obey Rule No 4

Option E – Correct: - This shape obeys all above stated rules

Hence Option E is Correct.

Question No 11.

Rule No 1. This matrix has a star-based pattern

Rule No 2. The outer boxes of the big upright triangle have three different shapes

Rule No 3. The outer boxes of the big upright triangle have different filling patterns on the upper portion and the same filling pattern on the lower portion

Rule No 4. The outer boxes of the big downward triangle have three different shapes

Rule No 5. The outer boxes of the big downward triangle have different filling patterns on the lower portion and the same filling pattern on the upper portion

Rule No 6. The inside hexagon has the same pattern in 3 adjacent triangles

Rule No 7. Inside the hexagon, 3 adjacent triangles with the same filling pattern have different shapes inside with no duplication

Rule No 8. Size/rotation/appearance/direction of inside shapes do not change.

Option A – Incorrect: - Does not obey Rule No 6

Option B – Correct: - This shape obeys all above stated rules

Option C – Incorrect: - Does not obey Rule No 6&7

Option D – Incorrect: - Does not obey Rule No 8

Option E – Incorrect: - Does not obey Rule No 7&8

Hence Option B is Correct.

Question No 12.

Rule No 1. This matrix has a star-based pattern

Rule No 2. Both big triangles have shape same appearance and filling design in opposite triangles pointing outward

Rule No 3. Inside hexagon has the same shapes in opposite triangles

Rule No 4. Size/rotation/appearance/direction of inside shapes do not change.

Option A – Incorrect: - Does not obey Rule No 2

Option B – Incorrect: - Does not obey Rule No 2

Option C – Correct: - This shape obeys all above stated rules

Option D – Incorrect: - Does not obey Rule No 3

Option E – Incorrect: - Does not obey Rule No 4

Hence Option C is Correct.

Question No 13.

Rule No 1. This matrix has a star-based pattern

Rule No 2. The outer boxes of the big upright triangle have the same shapes with a circle on the outside edge

Rule No 3. The outer boxes of the big upright triangle are unfilled

Rule No 4. The outer boxes of the big downward triangle have the same shapes with a circle on the outside edge

Rule No 5. The outer boxes of the big downward triangle are filled with a solid grey colour

Rule No 6. The inside hexagon has 3 adjacent filled triangles and 3 unfilled triangles

Rule No 7. Size/rotation/appearance/direction of inside shapes do not change.

Option A – Correct: - This shape obeys all above stated rules

Option B – Incorrect: - Does not obey Rule No 5

Option C – Incorrect: - Does not obey Rule No 4

Option D – Incorrect: - Does not obey Rule No 5

Option E – Incorrect: - Does not obey Rule No 7

Hence Option A is Correct.

Question No 14.

Rule No 1. This matrix has a star-based pattern

Rule No 2. The outer boxes of the big upright triangle have the same shapes

Rule No 3. The outer boxes of the big downward triangle have the same shapes

Rule No 4. Inside the hexagon, opposite triangles have different shapes (heart or pentagon)

Rule No 5. Size/rotation/appearance/direction of inside shapes do not change.

Option A – Correct: - This shape obeys all above stated rules

Option B – Incorrect: - Does not obey Rule No 4

Option C – Incorrect: - Does not obey Rule No 4

Option D – Incorrect: - Does not obey Rule No 4

Option E – Incorrect: - Does not obey Rule No 5

Hence Option A is Correct.

Question No 15.

Rule No 1. This matrix has a star-based pattern

Rule No 2. The outer boxes of the big upright triangle have the same shapes with the same filling pattern

Rule No 3. The outer boxes of the big downward triangle have the same shapes and are unfilled

Rule No 4. Inside the hexagon, 3 adjacent triangles have the same shape and same filling pattern

Rule No 5. Size/rotation/appearance/direction of inside shapes do not change.

Option A – Incorrect: - Does not obey Rule No 2

Option B – Incorrect: - Does not obey Rule No 5

Option C – Incorrect: - Does not obey Rule No 2

Option D – Correct: - This shape obeys all above stated rules

Option E – Incorrect: - Does not obey Rule No 2

Hence Option D is Correct.

NVR : Codes

Question No 1.

Rule No 1. The upper letter describes the type of shape

T=Pentagon

R=Cross Sign

E=Circle

W=Heart

Rule No 2. The lower letter describes the type of border it has

B=Thick solid

V=Dotted

C=Free hand made

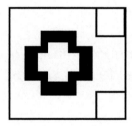

According to the above rules and keeping the above shape in mind, the correct option should have "R" on the upper side and "B" on the lower side.

Hence Option E is Correct.

Question No 2.

Rule No 1. The upper letter describes the filling pattern of the shape present inside the diamond

Z=Unfilled

A=Filled with solid black colour

Rule No 2. The lower letter describes the type of shape present in the diamond

J=Heart

K=4-point star

L=Triangle

According to the above rules and keeping the above shape in mind, the correct option should have "A" on the upper side and "K" on the lower side.

Hence Option C is Correct.

Question No 3.

Rule No 1. The upper letter describes the number of arrows in the shape

F=Four

T=Two

X=One

Rule No 2. The lower letter describes the size of arrows in the shape

B=Big

C=Small

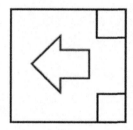

According to the above rules and keeping the above shape in mind, the correct option should have "X" on the upper side and "B" on the lower side.

Hence Option B is Correct.

Question No 4.

Rule No 1. The upper letter describes the type of shape

P=Circle

O=Smiley

U= Pentagon

Y=Sun

Rule No 2. The lower letter describes the number of shapes in the option

A=Three

S=Two

D=One

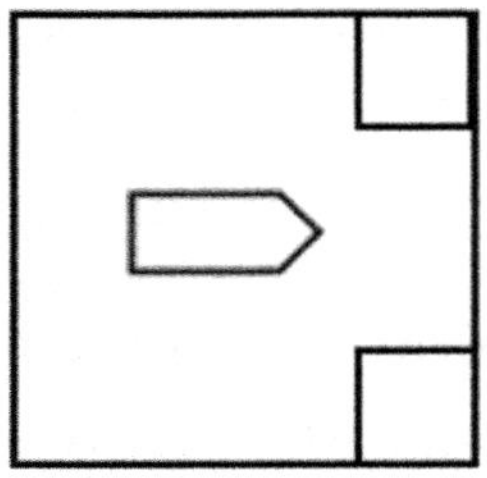

According to the above rules and keeping the above shape in mind, the correct option should have "U" on the upper side and "D" on the lower side.

Hence Option D is Correct.

Question No 5.

Rule No 1. The left letter describes the number of balls in the shape

X=Four

Y=Three

Z= Two

Rule No 2. The right letter describes the filling pattern of the lower left ball

Q=Filled with solid black

W=Filled with chess pattern

E=Filled with horizontal lines

R=Filled with downward diagonals

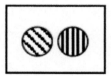

According to the above rules and keeping the above shape in mind, the correct option should have "Z" on the left side and "R" on the right side.

Hence Option D is Correct.

Question No 6.

Rule No 1. The left letter describes the filled pattern of the shape

A=Filled with dots

B=Filled with solid grey

C= Empty

Rule No 2. The right letter describes the filling pattern of the lower left ball

D=Z-type double side arrow with straight line double side arrow

L=Horizontal line double side arrow with diagonal double side arrow

Two diagonal double-side arrows

K= Horizontal line double side arrow with diagonal single side arrow

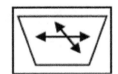

According to the above rules and keeping the above shape in mind, the correct option should have "C" on the left side and "L" on the right side.

Hence Option B is Correct.

Question No 7.

Rule No 1. The left letter describes the type of shape

A=Trapezoid

S=Parallelogram

D= Rectangle

F= Oval

G= Pentagon

Rule No 2. The right letter describes the filling pattern of the right side ball

H=Filled with vertical lines

J=Filled with downward diagonals

K=Filled with waves

M=Filled with horizontal lines

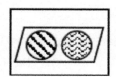

According to the above rules and keeping the above shape in mind, the correct option should have "S" on the left side and "K" on the right side.

Hence Option C is Correct.

Question No 8.

Rule No 1. The left letter describes the type of shape in the option

D=4-point star

Y=Diamond

T=Cross

M=Sun

Rule No 2. The right letter describes the position of the black triangle in the option

R=Half inside and half outside the shape

Q=Completely inside the Shape

P=Partial inside or outside the shape

According to the above rules and keeping the above shape in mind, the correct option should have "M" on the left side and "P" on the right side.

Hence Option A is Correct.

Question No 9.

Rule No 1. The left letter describes the number of lines and arrows in the shape

V=Four

B=Six

N=Five

Rule No 2. The right letter describes the number of double-sided arrows in the option

J=One

K=Three

L=Two

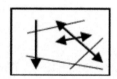

According to the above rules and keeping the above shape in mind, the correct option should have "B" on the left side and "L" on the right side.

Hence Option E is Correct.

Question No 10.

Rule No 1. The left letter describes type of the shape

G=L-type

H=Horizontal reflection of L=Type

Rule No 2. The right letter describes the filling pattern of both hearts

A=Both are unfilled

D=Upper unfilled lower filled

S=Upper filled lower unfilled

According to the above rules and keeping the above shape in mind, the correct option should have "H" on the left side and "D" on the right side.

Hence Option C is Correct.

Question No 11.

Rule No 1. The left letter describes the type of shape

C=Hexagon

V=Diamond

B=Pentagon

Rule No 2. The middle letter describes the division of the shape

A=Divided into two equal parts

D=Divided into quarter part

Rule No 3. The right letter describes the filling pattern of the shape

Y=Filled with solid black

Z=Filled with horizontal lines

According to the above rules and keeping the above shape in mind, the correct option should have "V" on the left side, "A" in the middle and "Z" on the right side.

Hence Option E is Correct.

Question No 12.

Rule No 1. The left letter describes the direction of the arrow positioned at the lower side of the shape

Y=Facing left

X=Facing right

Rule No 2. The middle letter describes the filling pattern of the left half

D=Vertical lines

A=Solid black

B=Diagonal bricks

Rule No 3. The right letter describes the filling pattern of the right half

N=Diagonal lines

O=Chess pattern

P=Waves

According to the above rules and keeping the above shape in mind, the correct option should have "Y" on the left side, "B" in the middle and "O" on the right side.

Hence Option D is Correct.

Question No 13.

Rule No 1. The left letter describes the sign inside the hexagon

A=Cross

B=Plus

Rule No 2. The middle letter describes the type and direction of the arrow

Z=Solid line facing right

Y=Solid line facing diagonal down

X=Dotted line facing right

V=Dotted line facing diagonal down

Rule No 3. The right letter describes the direction of the smiley face

P=Straight

Q=Inverted

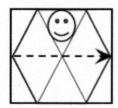

According to the above rules and keeping the above shape in mind, the correct option should have "A" on the left side, "X" in the middle and "P" on the right side.

Hence Option B is Correct.

Question No 14.

Rule No 1. The left letter describes the filled pattern of the hearts

P=Unfilled

Q=Filled with solid black

Rule No 2. The right letter describes the filling pattern of other shape

A=Horizontal bricks

S=Diagonal bricks

R=Waves

According to the above rules and keeping the above shape in mind, the correct option should have "P" on the left side and "S" on the right side.

Hence Option C is Correct.

Question No 15.

Rule No 1. The left letter describes the position and direction of the Pentagon

A=Up facing right

B=Down facing left

C=Down facing right

D=Up facing left

Rule No 2. The middle letter describes the direction of the arrows

F=Two arrows facing down

G=Four arrows facing down

H=Side arrows facing down and middle arrow facing up

J= Side arrows facing up and middle arrow facing down

Rule No 3. The right letter describes the filling pattern of the shape

Q=Vertical lines

W=Diagonal lines

E=Diagonal bricks

R=Chess pattern

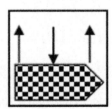

According to the above rules and keeping the above shape in mind, the correct option should have "C" on the left side, "J" in the middle and "R" on the right side.

Hence Option E is Correct.

NVR : Hidden Shapes

1. D because you can see the shape hidden under the curved arrow

2. A because the shape has only been rotated 90 degrees anti-clockwise and hidden under two rectangles

3. B because it has been rotated 180 degrees and hidden under two other shape

4. C because the shape in c is a circle with four lines coming out of the sides with nothing in the circle

5. C because the shape can be seen inside of the upside down pentagon with a triangle on top of it

6. E because if we take away the two quadrilaterals in front of the arrow and remove the square behind it we can see the shape

7. B because you can see that the shape is inside the circle

8. C because the shape has been rotated 90 degrees anti-clockwise

9. E because the shape has been rotated slightly anti-clockwise

10. E because nothing has been done to the shape (it is not b because b has a more circular shape)

11. D because the shape has been rotated 180 degrees clockwise

12. C because the central hexagon is connected with the same space as the three in the original shape

13. E because if you take away the two extra diamond shapes on the top the shape will be revealed

14. D because the shape has only just been rotated slighty clockwise

15. B because the shape has only just been rotated 90 degrees anti-clockwise and surrounded by a black circle

16. C because you can see that the shape has only just been hidden by a oval, triangle and two other long arrows

17. A because the shape has been kept as it is but other shapes have just been piled on top of it

18. E because you can see of the bottom two stars were to be removed and the floating two stars were to be removed the shape would be revealed

19. E because the shape has been kept the same but other shapes have been piled on top of it

20. C because if you remove the black arrows the shape will be revealed

21. B because the shape has only just been rotated 90 degrees clockwise and a rectangle, circle and extra pentagon has been added to the shape

NVR: Combination Shapes

1. In A, the line from the arrow is too short. In B, the shape is too big in width. In D, there is no rectangle in the main shape. In E, the arrow head is touching the rectangle- there is meant to be a short distance between them. Therefore, it's C.

2. In B, the star is different. In C, the additional shape with the smiley face isn't there. In D, the smiley face is the wrong way. In E, the shape attached to the smiley face is too short. That makes it A.

3. In A, the cylinder is incorrectly flipped. In B, there is a star instead of a heart. In C, there are arrow heads in each line- one line is meant to be empty. In E, the arrow heads are also wrongly placed. So, it's D.

4. In A, C and E, the main shape is incorrectly rotated. In D, the diamonds filling is white- it's meant to be black. It is B.

5. In A, the white arrow is going through the main shape whereas it should be underneath. In B and D, the diamond is white- should be black. In C, the main shape is incorrectly rotated. So, it is E.

6. In A, B and E, the diamonds on either side of the main shape have turned into squares. In D, the main shape is wrongly rotated. So, it is C

NVR : Folding and Punching Holes

Question No 1.

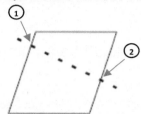

Rule No 1. Point No. 1 marked with a red arrow should be a common point at the upper side after folding

Rule No 2. Point No. 2 marked with a red arrow should be a common point at the lower side after folding

Rule No 3. After folding, the size of the folded part below this point should be the same as the above size before folding

Option A – Incorrect: - The folded part is transparent

Option B – Incorrect: - Does not obey Rule No 3

Option C – Correct: - This shape obeys all above stated rules

Option D – Incorrect: - Does not obey Rule No 1

Option E – Incorrect: - Does not obey Rule No 1

Hence Option C is Correct.

Question No 2.

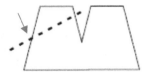

Rule No 1. The point marked with a red arrow should be a common point after folding

Rule No 2. After folding, the size of the folded part below the marked point should be the same as the above size before folding

Option A – Incorrect: - Does not obey Rule No 2

Option B – Correct: - This shape obeys all above stated rules

Option C – Incorrect: - Does not obey Rule No 1&2, irrelevant folding

Option D – Incorrect: - Does not obey Rule No 1&2, irrelevant folding

Option E – Incorrect: - Does not obey Rule No 1&2, irrelevant folding

Hence Option B is Correct.

Question No 3.

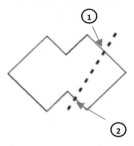

Rule No 1. Point No. 1 marked with a red arrow should be a common point at the upper side after folding

Rule No 2. Point No. 2 marked with a red arrow should be a common point at the lower side after folding

Rule No 3. After folding, the size of the folded part on the left side of the marked point No. 1 should be the same as the size on the right side before folding

Option A – Incorrect: - Does not obey Rule No 1

Option B – Incorrect: - Does not obey Rules No 1, 2 & 3. Irrelevant folding

Option C – Incorrect: - Does not obey Rule No 2

Option D – Incorrect: - Does not obey Rule No 3

Option E – Correct: - This shape obeys all above stated rules

Hence Option E is Correct.

Question No 4.

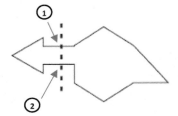

Rule No 1. Point No. 1 marked with a red arrow should be a common point at the upper side after folding

Rule No 2. Point No. 2 marked with a red arrow should be a common point at the lower side after folding

Rule No 3. After folding, the size of the folded part on the right side of the marked point No. 1 should be the same as the size on the left side before folding

Option A – Incorrect: - Does not obey Rule No 1&2

Option B – Incorrect: - Does not obey Rules No 1&2. Irrelevant folding

Option C – Incorrect: - Irrelevant folding

Option D – Correct: - This shape obeys all above stated rules

Option E – Incorrect: - Irrelevant folding

Hence Option D is Correct.

Question No 5.

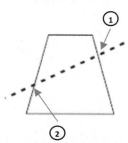

Rule No 1. Point No. 1 marked with a red arrow should be a common point at the upper side after folding

Rule No 2. Point No. 2 marked with a red arrow should be a common point at the lower side after folding

Rule No 3. After folding, the size of the folded part on the lower side of the marked point No. 1 should be the same as the size on the upper side before folding

Option A – Correct: - This shape obeys all above stated rules

Option B – Incorrect: - Does not obey Rule No 3

Option C – Incorrect: - Does not obey Rule No 1&2

Option D – Incorrect: - Does not obey Rule No 3

Option E – Incorrect: - Does not obey Rule No 1

Hence Option A is Correct.

Question No 6.

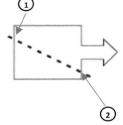

Rule No 1. Point No. 1 marked with a red arrow should be a common point at the upper side after folding

Rule No 2. Point No. 2 marked with a red arrow should be a common point at the lower side after folding

Rule No 3. After folding, the size of the folded part on the upper side of the marked point No. 1 should be the same as the size on the lower side before folding

Option A – Incorrect: - Does not obey Rule No 2

Option B – Incorrect: - Does not obey Rule No 1&2

Option C – Incorrect: - Irrelevant shape

Option D – Correct: - This shape obeys all above stated rules

Option E – Incorrect: - Does not obey Rule No 1&2

Hence Option D is Correct.

Question No 7.

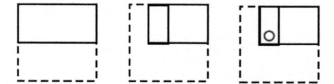

Rule No 1. Starting from the left, folding No. 1&2 is straight. Hence resultant holes should be in straight horizontal or vertical lines

Rule No 2. The number of layers at the punching point is four. Hence the number of holes in the resultant shape should be before i.e. 1x4=4 (hole layer rule)

Rule No 3. The punched hole is just touching the lower edge of the folding, hence the resultant shape should have: -

   (a) 2nd hole to the horizontal left of the punched hole

   (b) 3rd & 4th holes should be a vertical reflection of the above two holes

   (c) Distance between above row and lower row of holes should be minimum

Option A – Incorrect: - Does not obey Rule No 3a

Option B – Correct: - This option obeys all above stated rules

Option C – Incorrect: - Does not obey Rule No 3c

Option D – Incorrect: - Does not obey Rule No 3a

Option E – Incorrect: - Does not obey Rule No 3c

Hence Option B is Correct.

Question No 8.

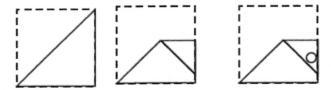

Rule No 1. Starting from the left, the first folding is diagonal and 2nd folding is straight down. Hence resultant holes should be straight vertical and diagonal

Rule No 2. The number of layers at the punching point is four. Hence the number of holes in the resultant shape should be before i.e. 1x4=4 (hole layer rule)

Rule No 3. The punched hole is just touching the lower edge of 2nd folding, hence the resultant shape should have: -

(a) 2nd hole is close to the upper right corner

(b) Remaining two holes with diagonal folding

Option A – Incorrect: - Does not obey Rule No 2

Option B – Incorrect: - Does not obey Rule No 3b

Option C – Correct: - This option obeys all above stated rules

Option D – Incorrect: - Does not obey Rule No 2

Option E – Incorrect: - Does not obey Rule No 3b

Hence Option C is Correct.

Question No 9.

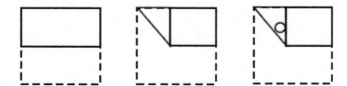

Rule No 1. Starting from left, 1st folding is straight up and 2nd folding is diagonal.

Rule No 2. The number of layers at the punching point is four. Hence the number of holes in the resultant shape should be before i.e. 1x4=4 (hole layer rule)

Rule No 3. The punched hole is just touching the lower edge of 2nd folding, hence the resultant shape should have: -

(a) 2nd hole should be on a diagonal left side to the punched hole

(b) The remaining two holes should be in vertical reflection of the above two holes

Option A – Incorrect: - Holes are at the irrelevant side

Option B – Incorrect: - Does not obey Rule No 3a

Option C – Incorrect: - Does not obey Rule No 2

Option D – Incorrect: - Does not obey Rule No 2

Option E – Correct: - This option obeys all above stated rules

Hence Option E is Correct.

Question No 10.

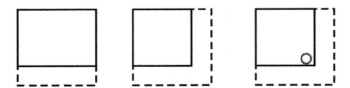

Rule No 1. Starting from left, 1st folding is straight up and 2nd folding is straight towards left. Hence resultant holes should be in straight horizontal or vertical lines

Rule No 2. The number of layers at the punching point is four. Hence the number of holes in the resultant shape should be before i.e. 1x4=4 (hole layer rule)

Rule No 3. The punched hole is just touching the lower edge of the folding, hence the resultant shape should have: -

(a) 2nd hole is just close to the right of the punched hole and

(b) Remaining two holes just beneath the above holes

Option A – Incorrect: - Does not obey Rule No 2

Option B – Incorrect: - Does not obey Rule No 2

Option C – Incorrect: - Does not obey Rule No. 3a, the distance between the left and the right column is more

Option D – Correct: - This option obeys all above stated rules

Option E – Incorrect: - Does not obey Rule No 2

Hence Option D is Correct.

Question No 11.

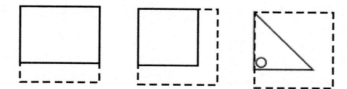

Rule No 1. Starting from the left, 1st folding is straight up, 2nd folding is straight towards the left and 3rd folding is diagonal downward to the left lower corner.

Rule No 2. The number of layers at the punching point is four. Hence the number of holes in the resultant shape should be before i.e. 1x4=4 (hole layer rule)

Rule No 3. The punched hole is just touching the lower left edge of the folding, hence the resultant shape should have:-

(a) 2nd hole is just in the opposite corner to the punched hole and

(b) 3rd hole in the upper right corner just close to the diagonal unfolded hole

(c) 4th hole should be just below the punched hole after de-folding all the layers

Option A – Incorrect: - Does not obey Rule No 2

Option B – Incorrect: - Does not obey Rule No 3c

Option C – Incorrect: - Does not obey Rule No 2

Option D – Correct: - This option obeys all above stated rules

Option E – Incorrect: - Does not obey Rule No 3b

Hence Option D is Correct.

Question No 12.

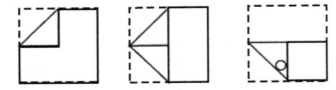

Rule No 1. Starting from the left, 1st folding is diagonally downward from the upper left corner, 2nd folding is diagonally upward from the lower left corner and 3rd folding is straight from upward to downward keeping the centre half common.

Rule No 2. The number of layers at the punching point is four. Hence the number of holes in the resultant shape should be before i.e. 1x4=4 (hole layer rule)

Rule No 3. The punched hole is just touching the lower right edge of the triangle folding, hence the resultant shape should have

(a) 2nd hole is just near the opposite upper line having the same distance as the punched hole with respect to the lower line

(b) 3rd hole to the diagonally a little upside to the previous hole just close to it

(c) 4th hole should be just to the left diagonally below the punched hole after de-folding all the layers

Option A – Incorrect: - Does not obey Rule No 2

Option B – Incorrect: - Does not obey Rule No 3a

Option C – Correct: - This option obeys all above stated rules

Option D – Incorrect: - Does not obey Rule No 3b

Option E – Incorrect: - Does not obey Rule No 3

Hence Option C is Correct.

Question No 13.

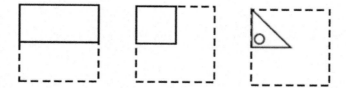

Rule No 1. Starting from left, 1st folding is vertically upward from the centre, 2nd folding is horizontally left from the centre and 3rd folding is diagonally downward from the right corner.

Rule No 2. The number of layers at the punching point is six. Hence the number of holes in the resultant shape should be before i.e. 1x8=8 (hole layer rule)

Rule No 3. The punched hole is just touching the lower left edge of the triangle folding, hence the resultant shape should have:-

(a) 2nd hole is in the opposite corner near the upper line

(b) 3rd hole to the horizontal right of the 2nd hole just close to it

(c) 4th hole to the horizontal right of the punched hole just close to the right line

(d) 5th, 6th, 7th & 8th holes should be the vertical reflection of the first four holes

Option A – Incorrect: - Does not obey Rule No 2

Option B – Incorrect: - Does not obey Rule No 2

Option C – Incorrect: - Has irrelevant distance between upper four holes and lower four holes

Option D – Incorrect: - Does not obey Rule No 2

Option E – Correct: - This option obeys all above stated rules

Hence Option E is Correct.

NVR : Nets and Cubes

Question No 1.

a   b   c   d   e

Option A – Correct: - This cube is a perfect result of folding the shape

Option B – Incorrect: - The dotted horizontal lines cannot be on the left side with respect to the triangle direction

Option C – Incorrect: - Diamond and triangle are in the opposite box, it is not possible to show them together

Option D – Incorrect: - The dotted horizontal lines cannot be on the left side when the diamond shape is on the upper side

Option E – Incorrect: - Dotted lines and solid black filled boxes are in the opposite box, it is not possible to show them together

Hence Option A is Correct.

Question No 2.

a   b   c   d   e

Option A – Incorrect: - The circle with the cross is mismatched shape, it is a plus sign instead.

Option B – Incorrect: - The upper side is empty, which is mismatched shape

Option C – Incorrect: - Diamond and chess-filled patterns are in the opposite box, it is not possible to show them together

Option D – Correct: - This cube is a perfect result of folding the shape

Option E – Incorrect: - Sun and solid black filled boxes are in the opposite box, it is not possible to show them together

Hence Option D is Correct.

Question No 3.

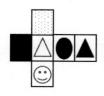

a   b   c   d   e

Option A – Incorrect: - Black circle and Black filled box are in the opposite box, it is not possible to show them together

Option B – Incorrect: - The black circle cannot be on the left side with respect to the triangle direction

Option C – Incorrect: - The black triangle cannot be on the left side of the circle with respect to the triangle direction

Option D – Incorrect: - Black triangle and white triangle are in the opposite box, it is not possible to show them together

Option E – Correct: - This cube is a perfect result of folding the shape

Hence Option E is Correct.

Question No 4.

a   b   c   d   e

Option A – Incorrect: - Sun and empty box are in the opposite box, it is not possible to show them together

Option B – Incorrect: - The sun cannot be on the upper side keeping in view the direction of the Pentagon

Option C – Incorrect: - Sun and empty box are in the opposite box, it is not possible to show them together

Option D – Incorrect: - Sun and empty box are in the opposite box, it is not possible to show them together

Option E – Correct: - This cube is a perfect result of folding the shape

Hence Option E is Correct.

Question No 5.

a   b   c   d   e

Option A – Correct: - This cube is a perfect result of folding the shape

Option B – Incorrect: - Black circle and smiley are in the opposite box, it is not possible to show them together

Option C – Incorrect: - Face is in the wrong direction with respect to the direction of the triangle

Option D – Incorrect: - Black-filled and chess-filled boxes are in the opposite box, it is not possible to show them together

Option E – Incorrect: - Empty box and triangle are in opposite boxes, it is not possible to show them together

Hence Option A is Correct.

Question No 6.

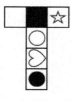

a   b   c   d   e

Option A – Correct: - This cube is a perfect result of folding the shape

Option B – Incorrect: - Black circle and white circle are in the opposite box, it is not possible to show them together

Option C – Incorrect: - Star and empty box are in the opposite box, it is not possible to show them together

Option D – Incorrect: - Black filled box and heart are in the opposite box, it is not possible to show them together

Option E – Incorrect: - Black filled box and heart are in the opposite box, it is not possible to show them together

Hence Option A is Correct.

Question No 7.

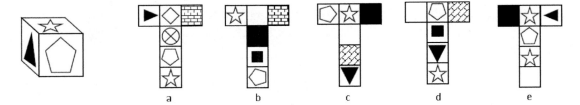

Option A – Incorrect: - The triangle is facing towards the diamond whereas it should face towards the star

Option B – Incorrect: - The triangle is not present in the options

Option C – Correct: - This cube is a perfect result of folding the shape

Option D – Incorrect: - The triangle and pentagon are in the opposite box, it is not possible to show them together

Option E – Incorrect: - It is not possible to have a triangle on the left side keeping in view the direction of the triangle and star in this option

Hence Option C is Correct.

Question No 8.

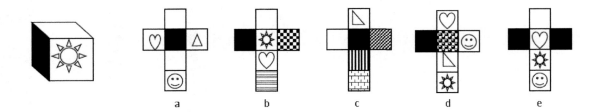

Option A – Incorrect: - The sun is not present in the shape

Option B – Correct: - This cube is a perfect result of folding the shape

Option C – Incorrect: - The sun is not present in the shape

Option D – Incorrect: - The empty box is not present in the shape

Option E – Incorrect: The empty box and the sun are in the opposite box, it is not possible to show them together

Hence Option B is Correct.

Question No 9.

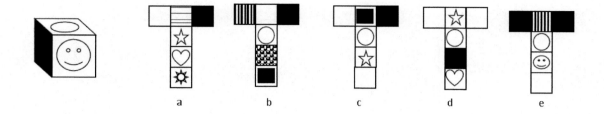

Option A – Incorrect: - The smiley is not present in the shape

Option B – Incorrect: - The smiley is not present in the shape

Option C – Incorrect: - The smiley is not present in the shape

Option D – Incorrect: - The smiley is not present in the shape

Option E – Correct: - This cube is a perfect result of folding the shape

Hence Option E is Correct.

Question No 10.

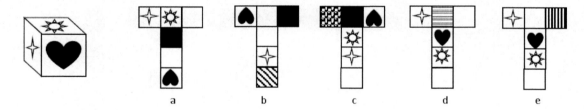

Option A – Incorrect: The direction of the heart is wrong

Option B – Incorrect: - The sun is not present in the shape

Option C – Correct: - This cube is a perfect result of folding the shape

Option D – Incorrect: The direction of the heart is wrong, it is facing towards the sun

Option E – Incorrect: The direction of the heart is wrong, it is facing towards the sun

Hence Option C is Correct.

Question No 11.

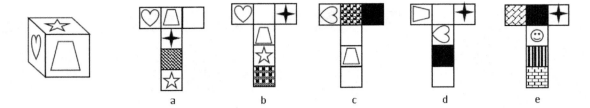

Option A – Correct: - This cube is a perfect result of folding the shape

Option B – Incorrect: - The direction of the star towards the pentagon is wrong

Option C – Incorrect: - The star is not present in the shape

Option D – Incorrect: - The star is not present in the shape

Option E – Incorrect: - The star is not present in the shape

Hence Option A is Correct.

Question No 12.

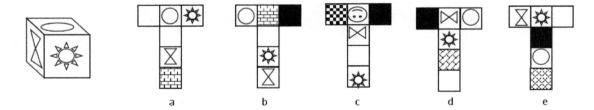

Option A – Incorrect: - The circle and Double triangles are in the opposite box, it is not possible to show them together

Option B – Incorrect: - The direction of the double triangle with respect to the sun is wrong

Option C – Incorrect: - Circle is not present in the shape

Option D – Correct: - This cube is a perfect result of folding the shape

Option E – Incorrect: - The sun and the circle are in the opposite box, it is not possible to show them together

Hence Option D is Correct.

Question No 13.

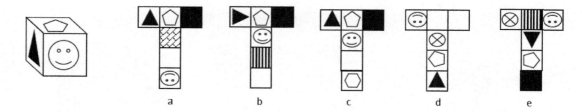

Option A – Incorrect: - The direction of pentagon with respect to the smiley is wrong

Option B – Correct: - This cube is a perfect result of folding the shape

Option C – Incorrect: - The direction of the triangle with respect to the pentagon is wrong

Option D – Incorrect: - The direction of the triangle with respect to the smiley is wrong

Option E – Incorrect: - The direction of the triangle with respect to the smiley is wrong

Hence Option B is Correct.

Question No 14.

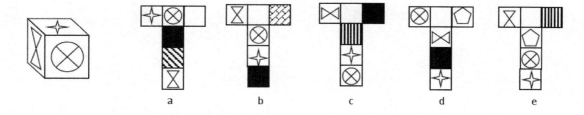

Option A – Incorrect: - The direction of the double triangle is wrong with respect to the circle

Option B – Incorrect: - The double triangle cannot be on the left side while keeping the 4-edge star at upside

Option C – Correct: - This cube is a perfect result of folding the shape

Option D – Incorrect: - The 4-edge star and the double triangles are in the opposite box, it is not possible to show them together

Option E – Incorrect: - The double triangle cannot be on the left side while keeping the 4-edge star at upside

Hence Option C is Correct.

Question No 15.

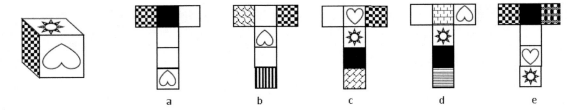

Option A – Incorrect: - The sun is not present in the shape

Option B – Incorrect: - The sun is not present in the shape

Option C – Correct: - This cube is a perfect result of folding the shape

Option D – Incorrect: - The chess-style filled box is not present in the shape

Option E – Incorrect: - The chess-style filled box cannot be on the left side while keeping the sun on the upper box

Hence Option C is Correct.

Question No 16.

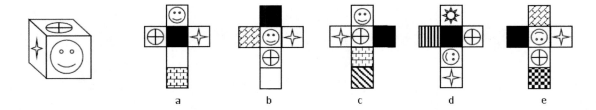

Option A – Incorrect: - 4-side star and circle are in the opposite box, it is not possible to show them together

Option B – Incorrect: - 4-side star cannot be on the left side while keeping the smiley upright

Option C – Incorrect: The direction of the smiley with respect to the circle is wrong

Option D – Incorrect: - The direction of the smiley is wrong with respect 4-side star

Option E – Correct: - This cube is a perfect result of folding the shape

Hence Option E is Correct.

NVR Spatial Reasoning : 2D Views

1. The blocks, when viewed from the left, forms an L shape. You can eliminate B, C and E. The L shape in option A is the wrong way. Therefore, it is D.

2. The blocks are a vertically straight line when viewed from the left side.
So, it must be B.

3. The blocks are vertically straight again but this time there are 3 additional blocks sticking out from the sides. One is from the top right. Another is from the botttom right. the last one is coming from the bottom left. So, it must be E.

4. The 2 blocks at the front form a line going upwards. There is one block sticking out fom the bottom right when viewed from the left side. That makes it D.

5. In the middle of the shape, there are 3 blocks. You take that as the base of the shape. So, it can't be D. At the second level, there are 2 blocks which are next to each other. Eliminate A and E. At the top, there is 1 block at the top left. Therefore it's C.

NVR Spatial Reasoning : 3D Building Blocks

1. There is 1 straight line block, 1 L shaped block and 1 T shaped block. Those blocks are in option B.

2. There is 1 cube block, and 2 L shaped blocks- one being shorter than the other. The best answer is D.

3. There is 1 T shaped block, 1 straight line block and 1 L shaped block. The best answer is C.

4. There is 2 L shaped blocks- each different lengths, 2 straight line blocks- one being shorter than the other. The answer is therefore E.

5. There is 2 L shaped blocks- different lengths, and 1 T shaped block. C is the best answer.

NVR Spatial Reasoning : 3D Rotation

1. Identify the notable feature in the shape. There are 2 cubes attached to either side of one of the straight line blocks. That applies in D only.

2. There is a bridge shape forming with a cube in it. That is in E.

3. There is only 1 cube block in this shape. Therefore, it's B.

4. There are only 4 blocks in this shape. That means it is A.

5. The only options left are F and C. This shape only has 2 cubes. That means it's F.

6. The remaining option is C.

Printed in Great Britain
by Amazon

46139756R00106